Let's Go Down to the Potter's House

JOANNE PUTNAM

Other Titles By Joanne Putnam

A Time to Grow
Growing in All the Right Places
So You Want to Write

Let's Go Down to the Potter's House

JOANNE PUTNAM

WORD AFLAME PRESS
8855 Dunn Road, Hazelwood, MO 63042
www.pentecostalpublishing.com

LET'S GO DOWN TO THE POTTER'S HOUSE

by Joanne Putnam

© 2006 Word Aflame Press
Hazelwood MO 63042-2299
Cover design and layout by Simeon Young Jr.

Printed in the United States of America

WORD AFLAME PRESS
8855 Dunn Road, Hazelwood, MO 63042
www.pentecostalpublishing.com

Library of Congress Cataloging-in-Publication Data

Putnam, Joanne.
    Let's go down to the Potter's House / by Joanne Putnam.
        p.   cm.
    ISBN-13: 978-1-56722-693-5
    1. Christian life. I. Title.
BV4501.3.P88 2006
248.4—dc22   2006020346

C O N T E N T S

INTRODUCTION

The prophet Jeremiah was sent "down to the potter's house" to receive a message from the Lord. It was a message that continues to apply to God's people today.

Jeremiah watched as the potter molded and shaped a vessel on his wheel. The Lord told Jeremiah to tell His chosen people that they were to be like clay in the hand of the potter, willing to be fashioned by the Master for whatever purpose seemed best to Him.

The Lord Jesus Christ continually desires to mold people's lives as it seems best to Him. *Let's Go Down to the Potter's House* contains thoughts, messages, and encouragement to help people remain pliable in the Master's hands as He makes them and molds them into vessels He can use for His glory, vessels of honor, made in His image and likeness.

My greatest desire is to inspire you to grow spiritually in every aspect of your life, as you walk humbly with your God.

Let's Go Down to the Potter's House

CHAPTER ONE

Let's Go Down to the Potter's House

$\mathcal{F}$or some reason art class at Mason Elementary School stands out in my mind. Our art teacher was Mrs. Glocar, a tall, thin, blonde-haired lady with a glass eye.

I'm sure I had Mrs. Glocar for several years, but fourth-grade art class was the most memorable. We had art on Thursday, and that became my favorite day of the week. I remember having a certain fall-colored dress that I always wore on Thursday because I thought it was so pretty. Now that I think about it, poor Mrs. Glocar probably thought that was the only dress I had!

In the fall of fourth grade, Mrs. Glocar showed us how to use pastels and how to blend the chalky colors. We made beautiful autumn scenes. I've never forgotten that because, for the first and only time in my life, my picture was hung on the wall in the hall for everyone to see. My one and only artistic accomplishment worthy of "publication."

In the spring of that year, she introduced us to clay. She showed us the basics of making clay and gave us the freedom to create whatever we wanted to make. I decided to make a lamb figurine for my mom for Mother's Day. I remember the concern of the teacher as to whether the lamb could remain standing through the firing process because of the weight of the body on the thin legs. I was so relieved when it came out of the kiln and was still standing! I was so proud of that lamb!

We recently built a new church. In the process of moving, we changed the name to The Potter's House. The name change drew me to potters and pottery. Just as in my art class years ago, I was fascinated that a potter can take a gray or brown or red lump of clay, shape it and form it, put it into a hot oven to bake, and turn it into a beautiful, decorative and useful piece of art.

If you've ever watched potters at work, you can't help but note how easy they make it look. They throw clay on their wheels and skillfully manipulate it with the touch of their fingers as it spins around and around.

Not long ago, I was afforded the opportunity to closely observe a potter at work. It was amazing to watch her as she "threw" clay on the wheel and, with seemingly simple moves of her hands, formed the malleable substance into various bowls and vases. As we watched, she explained what she was doing. She told us that some pots go exactly as planned. They take shape beautifully and quickly and in no time at all are ready for firing. She told us that some pieces start well but end up leaning the wrong way. If that happens, she has to stop the process and take them off the wheel, rework them and put them on the wheel again. She said that sometimes, as she is working on a piece, she finds that the clay isn't really ready to be shaped. It might have air bubbles in it or hard pieces that haven't been broken down to allow it to be molded properly, so it has to go back in the bucket to have more preparation.

It was fascinating to see a master potter at work.

Making our own pottery isn't something that we need to be concerned about today. We can go to the store and buy just about every type of receptacle you can imagine. In Bible days, one didn't have such luxury. If a woman didn't have durable clay pots, she couldn't function on a daily basis. It would be the equivalent of not having any plastic storage pieces in your kitchen today. How would you function without all those whipped topping bowls and soft butter tubs? Imagine no Rubbermaid or Tupperware!

In the Old and New Testaments, clay pots were used to hold and carry water, to store things in, to wash in, and to cook in. Jesus used parables, stories that the people could understand, to help them comprehend His word. He wanted Israel to know who their God and creator was, and because they understood the importance of clay pots, He showed them the workings of a potter:

> *The word which came to Jeremiah from the LORD, saying, Arise, and go down to the potter's house, and there I will cause thee to hear my words. Then I went down to the potter's house, and, behold, he wrought a work on the wheels. And the vessel that he made of clay was marred in the hand of the potter: so he made it again another vessel, as seemed*

*good to the potter to make it. Then the word of the LORD
came to me, saying, O house of Israel, cannot I do with you
as this potter? saith the LORD. Behold, as the clay is in the
potter's hand, so are ye in mine hand, O house of Israel.*
(Jeremiah 18:1-6)

In Jeremiah 19, the Lord gave Jeremiah an object lesson to
share with the people. He told Jeremiah to buy a clay pot and to
break it in front of the leaders of Israel and warn them what was
to come if they continued to worship false gods. Jesus was using
what they understood to remind them that just as a potter forms
items from clay, He had formed them from the dust of the earth,
and if they weren't willing to obey Him, He could destroy them
as easily as He had created them.

*Thus saith the LORD, Go and get a potter's earthen bot-
tle, and take of the ancients of the people, and of the ancients
of the priests; And go forth unto the valley of the son of
Hinnom, which is by the entry of the east gate, and proclaim
there the words that I shall tell thee.* (Jeremiah 19:1-2)

*Then shalt thou break the bottle in the sight of the men
that go with thee, and shalt say unto them, Thus saith the
LORD of hosts; Even so will I break this people and this city,
as one breaketh a potter's vessel, that cannot be made
whole again.* (Jeremiah 19:10-11)

Let's Go Down to the Potter's House

There are many other Scriptures in the Bible that refer to us as clay in the Master's hands:

Remember, I beseech thee, that thou hast made me as the clay; and wilt thou bring me into dust again? (Job 10:9)

But now, O LORD, thou art our father; we are the clay, and thou our potter; and we all are the work of thy hand. (Isaiah 64:8)

Hath not the potter power over the clay, of the same lump to make one vessel unto honour, and another unto dishonour? (Romans 9:21)

The verse of Scripture on which I would like you to focus is Jeremiah 18:2 "Arise, and go down to the potter's house, and there I will cause thee to hear my words."

There are still lessons to be learned by "going down to the potter's house," even in this modern day in which we live.

I did that just recently as I was preparing this thought. I had done some research on clay and pottery making and then I stopped by a local clay company to see if I could buy some clay. I only wanted a pound or two so I could use it as a visual aid, but the man informed me that they only sold it in twenty-five-pound bags. I told him I only needed a little and I told him it was to help me give a message about our being the clay and God being the potter. He said, "Hold on a minute." He went back into the building, reached into the mixer as it was being processed, and brought me a rather large lump of clay for which he wouldn't let me pay. He told me that the owner's brother was a pastor and that he was sure he wouldn't mind giving me some!

He proceeded to give me some information about the clay. He said that the clay he had given to me was a dark clay when it was fired and that it had a lot of iron in it. He also told me that if anyone did want to fire it, it should be fired at cone 5 because of the ingredients that had been added to it. I would have had no clue as to what that meant had I not done some research.

Did you know that clay is made from decomposed granite rock? What is granite like? Hard! That's why, when it is fired, it becomes hard and non-porous. It is a mixture of several substances, and impurities are always present.

Did you know that when raw clay is dug from the ground, it isn't ready to use? Potters have a lot of work to do to get clay ready for use.

Before clay can be used, it has to be pure—or clean. It can't have any impurities in it. Preparing clay for use is a lot of work! First it must be spread out to dry, preferably on wooden boards in the bright sun. When it is thoroughly dry, large lumps need to be pounded with a mallet or block of wood and broken up. Then the clay can be made into what they call "slip" by sifting it into a pail of water and allowing it to slake, or soak, for several hours. After the soaking process, it is put through a sieve to remove impurities. Oftentimes other ingredients, such as minerals, need to be added to get the potter's desired effect. Then it has to be mixed thoroughly.

Clay has to have the proper amount of water to reach the elasticity necessary to form or mold it. It has to be kneaded to take out all the air pockets, and it has to have an even consistency.

Have you ever seen some of the potter's tools? When we think of potters we usually just think of two things: their hands and the potter's wheel. Potters actually have many tools that they use. One thing they use to help prepare the clay just before they put it on the wheel is a tool with a wire attached to a board. They do a process called "wedging," where they take the clay and smash it into the wire, literally cutting it in half over and over, and then they slam the pieces on top of each other. They do this about twenty times before they put it on their wheel or begin shaping it. This allows them to check the inside to make sure there are no air pockets or lumps in the middle. They have other tools they use: sharp sticks to punch and poke at the clay, scrapers, sponges to sop up excess water, wire-looped tools to gouge out pieces, and knives to cut into the clay. Clay is put through a very strenuous process before it is fit for use in the potter's hands.

To actually be useful, clay then has to be fired, or matured. One historian thinks that hardening clay by firing it was probably discovered by accident. He said that someone had probably lined a basket with clay to hold a substance and accidentally dropped the basket into a fire where the warp was burned up, only to find that the clay had hardened and was capable of holding liquids.

The natural impurities of the clay affect its working proper-ties. Its aesthetic, or artistic value and use, is determined by the intensity of the heat needed to harden it. In other words, its beauty and usefulness are determined by both the quality of the clay and its ability to withstand heat.

There are four basic types of vessels that are made of clay: earthenware, stoneware, china, and porcelain. Each of these finished clays has a different use and is fired at a different temperature.

Earthenware, such as a clay pot, is fired at the mere temperature of 1500° to 1850° F. It is too porous to hold water unless it is glazed. It is very fragile and breaks easily.

Stoneware, such as a mug, is fired at 2200° F and is a little more durable than earthenware.

China, which makes a much finer, thinner piece, requires two or more firings at a much higher temperature than earthenware and stoneware.

Porcelain is fired at the hottest fire at 2500° to 2650° F and is made from a specially prepared mix of very fine clay. Clay that is useful for porcelain has had numerous poundings and siftings to make sure it is fine enough to be used. Porcelain is a durable, non-absorbent ceramic.

As I studied the process of preparing natural clay for use, I was amazed to learn the correlation between the preparation a potter uses to prepare natural clay for use and the spiritual preparation the master Potter uses to prepare us for spiritual use.

Just as clay is made of decomposed granite and full of impurities, when Jesus digs us from the earth of life, we are full of decomposed, hard components and full of impurities. When we first come to Jesus, we are not ready to be used. Jesus has to take our hardened hearts and make us pliable, sensitive, and able to do

His will. At times we go through "dry" spells as He pounds us and seemingly grinds us to a pulp so He can purify us and cleanse us from our old ways. Oftentimes we feel as though we are being sifted and sieved and feel that we can't take any more, but Jesus said He would never leave us or forsake us and that He wouldn't give us more than we could bear. We feel Him kneading us, just as the potter kneads clay, as He takes the air pockets of pride out of us to make us realize that without Him, we are nothing.

To truly be a vessel God can use, we also have to go through the firing or maturing process. Just as no two common clays are alike, no two people are alike. Just as different clays react differently to the fire, so do we. We all have different situations that we face in life as we go through the firing process. Sometimes we don't take the firing process very well. Life isn't always what we want it to be. Sometimes we try to become our own potter and make life what we want it to be. We see others with their wealth and what seems like blessings, and we don't understand. The psalmist Asaph said that his foot almost slipped when he saw the prosperity of the wicked.

But as for me, my feet were almost gone; my steps had well nigh slipped. For I was envious at the foolish, when I saw the prosperity of the wicked. (Psalm 73:2-3)

What he was saying was that he almost took his life into his own hands when he saw it wasn't going as well as he thought it should be! In other words, he almost took his life off the Potter's wheel!

When we get frustrated and feel like we just can't take any more, we need to realize that we're not alone. We need to remind ourselves that it's all a part of the process and what the end result will be if we remain on His wheel.

Just as some of the potter's vessels don't make it to the finished product, unfortunately some of God's chosen people aren't going to make it either. Paul told Timothy that in the last days perilous times would come, that people would resist the truth, that they would be lovers of pleasure more than lovers of God and that they will become scoffers, walking after their own lusts. There will be people who once served God who will take control of their lives into their own hands and take themselves off the Potter's wheel.

Paul put it this way in Romans 10:3 "For they being ignorant of God's righteousness, and going about to establish their own righteousness, have not submitted themselves unto the righteousness of God."

The Amplified Bible version of Romans 10:3 says: "For being ignorant of the righteousness that God ascribes (which makes one acceptable to Him in word, thought, and deed), and seeking to establish a righteousness (a means of salvation) of their own, they did not obey or submit themselves to God's righteousness."

King Saul took himself off God's wheel when he disobeyed the Lord's divine instructions. Samuel the prophet was sent to tell King Saul that "to obey is better than sacrifice." No one, not even the king, is exempt from following God's perfect will.

Regardless of what we think we are doing for God, if we are not obedient to Him, it means nothing and we are going against His will. The Scriptures say, "To him that knoweth to do good, and doeth it not, to him it is sin" (James 4:17).

We need to leave our life in His hands. As He is the master Potter, we have to know and trust that He knows what is best for us on the wheel of life.

When we were in Germany, the first year we were there my husband went through a trial of depression that became so severe that at one point I had to literally pull him out of bed and make him go to church. This depression lasted for about nine months. When it was over, he said that his life felt like he had opened the manhole cover of a sewer and for nine months he had walked in the sewer. It was a fiery trial. He felt the heavens were brass and he felt that God was a million miles away.

One night he was on a train as he was returning home after a Bible study. He was deeply depressed, feeling his life was worthless, as he rode the train. As was his custom, he began talking to the Lord. He asked the Lord, "Lord, would you just make me the man you want me to be?"

Finally, after nine months of feeling that he had not heard His voice, he heard the Lord clearly speak to him and say, "So let me!" And He gave him this verse of Scripture:

He hath shewed thee, O man, what is good; and what doth the LORD require of thee, but to do justly, and to love mercy, and to walk humbly with thy God? (Micah 6:8)

21

God is trying to make you the person He wants you to be. Will you let Him? Clay that is being fired has no choice as to how hot the oven will get or what type of vessel the potter has destined it to become. That is not true of us. Our Potter has a plan and purpose for our lives, but He has given us the choice as to how long we will remain on His wheel and what type of vessel we will become. Which type of vessel would you like to be?

Would you like to be a clay pot, a stoneware mug, or a china cup? I believe that Jesus would have each of us be the finest piece of spiritual porcelain possible. The choice is up to us!

Could there be something that is keeping you from becoming what God truly would like you to become? Are you saturated with His Spirit enough to admit you have a need? Is there an air pocket of pride deep inside you? Is there a lump you are holding on to from the past that you aren't willing to let Him grind up? Is it that you feel the maturing process is too hot and you want to get out of the heat? Is it that you feel you may have to change some things in your life and you feel the cost of obedience is too high a price to pay? Perhaps you are unhappy with the vessel He is making of you?

Let me tell you something: if you have a Bible in your possession, whether you want to believe it or not, you are accountable for what it says. Pleading ignorance on the Day of Judgment will not give you the glory or mercy available on this side of eternity.

Whatever it may be that is keeping you from allowing God to mold you and make you into a vessel He can use: lay it aside. Lay it all down at the feet of the master Potter, the great Creator, and let Him make you the vessel He wants you to be.

One pottery book I read had these two profound statements in it:

"There is no thrill in pottery quite equal to that of digging your own clay, preparing it for use, and making something from it."

"When a potter works or 'throws' on his wheel there is magic in his touch. The clay comes to life in his hands as it rises from shapeless mass to forms of grace and elegance."

When I read that, all I could think of was the thrill Jesus must feel when He digs us out of the clay pit of life and with His touch allows us to come to life as He shapes us and prepares us for a vessel He can use.

Indeed Ephesians 2:10 is true, "For we are his workmanship, created in Christ Jesus unto good works, which God hath before ordained that we should walk in them."

To Be Used of God

CHAPTER TWO

To Be Used of God

*H*ave you ever prayed to be used of God? Have you ever prayed that God would take your life into His own hands and use you for His divine will and purpose in His kingdom?

Have you ever really considered what the statement "to be used of God" means?

For a moment I would like for you to think about the things you use in this life. Throughout a typical American day, we use a lot of things! We use rooms in our home, we use clothes, we use soaps, shampoos, hair dryers, cleaning supplies, lights, electricity, machines, appliances, vehicles, pencils, computers, paper, books. . . .

Some things we use are highly expendable. Like paper towels or soap, we use them once, then throw them in the trash or wash them down the drain.

Some things we use require very little maintenance. We may need to stack them, reorganize them, or clean them occasionally, but basically they just sit there with very little activity until we actually need to use them.

Some things we use require a lot of maintenance and are very "touchy." They require constant vigilance in making sure that they stay in good working order. Often these are the big-ticket items that we feel we just must have—but we don't use them nearly as much as we thought we would, and we end up having to learn again and again how to use them! Or we end up using them as very expensive coatracks because we don't make the time to use them like we know we should. (Exercise equipment!)

Some things we use are recyclable. Plastics, cardboard, oils, steel, water—they're even working on ways to recycle our garbage so we don't have so many landfills. Things can be cleansed, reformed, reformatted, and restructured to be used over and over in different capacities.

So what does "use" mean?

- As a noun it means employ, exercise, utilization, application, consumption, benefit, avail, and service.
- As a verb it means to make use of, put into operation, set in motion, set to work, work, exert, exercise, take up, try to bring into play, use up, consume, expend, be spent, tax, task, help, aid, and to discharge a function.
- As an adjective it means to be instrumental, utilitarian, subservient, employable, valuable, productive, effectual, effective, available, and workable.

Being used expends energy. It is work!

To Be Used of God

We sing that old song, "To Be Used of God," but do we think of the ramifications of what we are singing?

Some of the synonyms for work sound pretty good: utilize, employ, benefit, available, but what about the ones that say work! exert! exercise! expend! subservient! Ow!

God truly wants to use us, and He will if we just allow Him to!

I Corinthians 12:28 tells us: "And God hath set some in the church, first apostles, secondarily prophets, thirdly teachers, after that miracles, then gifts of healings, helps, governments, diversities of tongues."

So often we think that for God to use us, either we have to be in a certain spiritual condition or that the task He calls us to do has to be magnificent for it to count. That just is not true!

God has given the church certain leadership positions, but we are not all called to be those leaders. Not all of us are needed to preach crusades to hundreds of thousands of people in Ethiopia like Reverend Billy Cole.

There are other gifts that we can all do and participate in. One of the gifts He has given is the gift of "helps." I think this is one of those words that we all just skim over as we read this text. The gift of helps is a gift that everyone can and should participate in.

God wants to use each of us where we are and with the resources we personally have available, even though we may not think it is very much. He wants us to do the things we can do for Him now!

Maybe you can't talk to one hundred people every day, but

you could pray with the coworker who just told you he is sick or bring him to church like the four friends who carried their friend to Jesus and ended up taking the tiles off the roof to get him inside where Jesus was. You can demonstrate your faith to those you meet every day as you show people kindness by what you say and what you do: a smile, a kind word, a compliment.

You can be like the servant girl who told Naaman where he needed to go to see the prophet in order to be healed of leprosy.

You can be like the widow who chose to feed the prophet, knowing that she had so little food that there would probably be nothing left for her and her son.

You could be like the good Samaritan who stopped to care for a dying man whom many people passed because they were too busy and didn't want to get their hands dirty.

You could be like the Shunammite woman who had a burden for the prophet, so she had her husband build a little room so the prophet would have a comfortable place to stay as he traveled through their land.

According to Matthew Henry's Commentary:

HELPS: It is a gift of ministry (I Corinthians 12:28). The helps of I Corinthians refers to the ability to offer help or assistance. It has been suggested that Paul refers to the ministry of the deacons who care for the poor and the sick. It is a general reference to all those who demonstrate love in their dealings with others.

To Be Used of God

So the gift of helps is actually demonstrating love, something we should be doing every day of our lives as we share the love of Christ. It is being available when a need arises, be it big or small. We are laborers together with Him when we help others.

For we are labourers together with God. (I Corinthians 3:9)

Therefore, my beloved brethren, be ye stedfast, unmoveable, always abounding in the work of the Lord, forasmuch as ye know that your labour is not in vain in the Lord. (I Corinthians 15:58)

Jesus will never ask you to do something beyond your reach. You may have to stretch when you take that first step, like the widow woman who fed the prophet first or the friends who had to take the tiles off the roof, but He will be right there.

Never fear that you can't do what He asks you to do: God always empowers whomever He employs! That means that He will never give you a task to do that is too great for you to accomplish, with His help.

Are you willing to let God use you? Unfortunately, sometimes we give God lip service. We say we are willing to be used, but when He calls upon us, we hesitate, just like the people who looked at the wounded man who had been beaten and robbed. We look at the need and run away quickly so we won't be pressed into service.

If you really desire to be used by God in the gift of helps, I do need to warn you about something. When you open yourself up to helping people—you also open yourself up to be hurt. When you help people, they don't always respond in the way you think they should. Kind of like the wounded animal that you tried to help that turned to bite you. You knew you were only trying to help, but the animal lashed out at you, thinking you were trying to hurt it. Sometimes that happens with people too! That's why, when you help someone, you have to realize that ultimately you are doing it for the Lord, and unfortunately that's how people treat Him too. Always keep in mind that when you help someone, you are doing the work for Him. You are His hands and feet.

So you've determined you want to be used by God; now the next question is: How will you respond when He uses you?

- Will you let Him use you like you use a paper towel, just throwing it in the trash and forgetting about it? What if, after you're used, you don't receive any personal credit for what you have done? There's no doubt about it, when we want to be used of God, we need to realize that work is involved and that we may never get credit for the things we have done. So if you're looking for "glory" and "rewards," you'll just have to wait until you get to heaven!
- Are you willing to sit on the shelf and wait, like some of the things we use, until He feels it is the right timing to use you, even though you may feel the timing is right now?
- Will you be like the "touchy" things we use that require

a lot of maintenance? Will you be offended if you aren't constantly told what a good job you've done? Will you fold yourself away like a piece of exercise equipment, putting yourself under a bed and pouting for a while?

- Are you willing to let God recycle you? Willing to be used again and again and again, in whatever capacity the Lord has need of? Being willing to do whatever job He needs you to do? It could be to take out the garbage at church. It could be to help clean up after a potluck. It could be to teach Sunday school. It could be to clean out your closet to give someone needed clothes. It could be to pick up people to come to church. It could be to sit with someone in the hospital while a loved one is in surgery. It could be to help someone at the checkout line who's run a little short of cash and just needs a couple of dollars to pay the rest of the bill so she won't have to put things back on the shelf. It could be to send a card in the mail telling someone you've been missing him at church and that you are praying for him. It could be to respond to an accident with emergency help. It could be to host a foreign exchange student to introduce her to the truth of God's Word. It could be to pray with a distraught coworker on the spur of the moment. It could be a pat on the back and word of encouragement to a friend. It could be to silently slip some cash into the hand of a brother or sister whom you know is having a difficult time.
- It could be teaching a Bible study.

- Sometimes it is just a kind word: "The Lord God hath given me the tongue of the learned, that I should know how to speak a word in season to him that is weary" (Isaiah 50:4).
- And the list goes on and on.

I think it is interesting that just three verses after the Word talks about the gift of helps is I Corinthians 13:1 "Though I speak with the tongues of men and of angels, and have not charity, I am become as sounding brass, or a tinkling cymbal."

And what is charity? Love. And what is love? God. The Lord Jesus Christ. It is we when we become His hands and feet, helping people in whatever capacity we can, and being available to help others so they can see the love of Christ working in us.

I beseech you, brethren, (ye know the house of Stephanas, that it is the firstfruits of Achaia, and that they have addicted themselves to the ministry of the saints,) that ye submit yourselves unto such, and to every one that helpeth with us, and laboureth. (I Corinthians 16:15-16)

Paul said that the house of Stephanas had "addicted themselves to the ministry of the saints" and then he told the readers of his letter, "Submit yourselves unto such, and to every one that helpeth with us, and laboureth."

If you truly are willing to allow God to use you to help people with the gift of helps:

- you don't care who gets the credit,
- you realize you could get your feelings hurt,
- and you are willing to allow God to use you in whatever capacity He will.

Take a moment right now to bow your head and ask the Lord: Lord, what would You have me do? Whom would You have me help today? How can I be used by You to accomplish the greatest work possible in these last days?

The Gift of Encouragement

CHAPTER THREE

The Gift of Encouragement

*W*as there something in your life that you really felt you could accomplish—but someone discouraged you from doing it?

Maybe it was a teacher who discouraged you from taking a course or going on to college, or perhaps it was a parent who discouraged you from taking a risk? Was it your husband or wife who discouraged you? Think for just a moment: What was it and who was it that discouraged you?

Did you make the decision as a result of their counsel not to do what you wanted to do or felt you could do, or did you decide you would try it anyway?

I'll never forget a story my grandmother told me. She had worked hard all of her life. She started out cooking at a logging camp in the hills of West Virginia, where she met my grandfather. After years of raising children and living and working on a farm, she had a dream to open her own restaurant in town, in her home, on a busy street in Akron, Ohio. She talked with my grandfather and told him her thoughts as she made plans as to how she would set it up, operate it and maintain it. Because their home was large and had two apartments upstairs, she planned for them to live upstairs and have the restaurant downstairs. She had the building inspector come out and they discussed how the kitchen would operate and where the separate restrooms would be located. She had everything ready to go and told my grandfather that the carpenter would be there the next day to cut the window for the kitchen. Up to this point he had listened to all of her plans and said basically nothing. He didn't discourage her and he didn't encourage her. He had let her do all the talking. When she informed him that the construction was ready to begin, he told her, "The day they cut the window is the day I move out."

End of the story! That was it! She didn't argue, she didn't cry, she didn't pout. It was over. He was a man of few words and she knew that he meant what he said. So that was that! Her dream was dead!

Florence Littauer, in her book *Silver Boxes*, shared a story about her father. One day when Florence was visiting him, he had her get a box from behind a chest of drawers that contained some letters and articles that he had written. When she began reading the letters and responses that he had received from people, she was totally amazed. She didn't understand why he had never shared this gift of writing with the family before. He told her that he had always dreamed of running for a political office but that his wife, her mother, had discouraged him from politics and from writing because he didn't have the formal education to warrant it. So he hid his dream.

I think all of us, to some degree, have had a dream that was destroyed by someone else. Some of us are "fighters" and we determine to make our dreams happen anyway, but not everyone is.

In this chapter I would like to share with you the concept of silver boxes, or the gift of encouragement.

Do you like to give or receive gifts? Do you realize that there are priceless gifts that you can give and receive every day that do not cost a penny, that can change the course of your life and the lives of those around you?

The words that we say can be a gift to those with whom we come in contact each day. Words are powerful. Words literally have the power of life and death. With our words we can curse a person or we can bless a person. Scriptures tell us that our words literally bring life and death to the hearer. Words can give hope or destroy hope.

Unfortunately, some of the cruelest words spoken are to those whom we should love the most, our family members.

Death and life are in the power of the tongue: and they that love it shall eat the fruit thereof. (Proverbs 18:21)

Out of the same mouth proceedeth blessing and cursing. My brethren [and sisters], these things ought not so to be. (James 3:10)

Proverbs 12:18 (NIV) says: "Reckless words pierce like a sword, but the tongue of the wise brings healing."

The way we react to a situation and what we blurt out reveal our inward heart. We may be trying to mask or hide our true feelings, but once the words are spoken, no amount of denying them can erase them. One writer said it is like toothpaste that has been squeezed from the tube; there is no way to put it back in the tube once it is out.

Out of the abundance of the heart the mouth speaketh. (Matthew 12:34)

We would interpret that to mean: What is in the well comes up in the bucket!

If our hearts are wells, what words would each of these hearts yield?

- Angry heart yields angry words
- Bitter heart yields bitter words
- Haughty (proud) heart yields haughty words
- Pessimistic heart yields pessimistic words
- Peaceful heart yields peaceful words
- Contented heart yields contented words
- Hopeful heart yields hopeful or encouraging words

Ephesians 4:29 tells us: "Let no corrupt communication proceed out of your mouth, but that which is good to the use of edifying, that it may minister grace unto the hearers."

Let's look at the meaning of the terms "minister" and

"grace." Minister means: to give, bestow, bring forth, deliver, or offer. Grace means: graciousness (as gratifying) of manner or action, especially the divine influence upon the heart and its reflection in the life; including gratitude: acceptable, benefit, favor, gift, grace, joy.

By definition then, the term "minister grace" is actually saying that our words should not only be positive but that they are to be gifts from the heart that we are to give to others, to edify them, to lift them up, to encourage them.

Let me repeat that: Our words should be gifts from the heart that we give to others to encourage them and to lift them up, not to put them down.

When we minister to people, we attempt to meet their deepest needs. When we minister grace to them, we should be trying to give them the same kind of understanding, forgiveness, and encouragement that Jesus gives us. What we say to others should be an encouragement and edification—words to lift them up.

Our words should be gifts from the heart that we generously give to people every day!

One little girl said that our words should be like silver boxes, a beautiful gift that we have wrapped in silver and placed a bow on top!

Our words should be beautiful gifts we give to one another, not offensive, hurtful, and unkind.

If I offered you a choice between a silver box and a box of garbage, which would you choose? Some words are like silver boxes, gifts to the hearer. Some words are like rotting garbage.

As you read through this list of words, in your mind decide: Would they be like silver boxes, or would they be like rotting garbage to the hearer's ears?

Blessing	Cursing
Life	Putdown
Healing	Piercing, cutting words
Encouragement	Discouragement
Compassion	Cynicism

We need to be encouragers every day with the words that we speak, not discouragers. We need to send our families out the door each day with the most positive feelings we can give them. We need to make our homes so cheerful and inviting that our family members can't wait to get back!

Unfortunately, there are often conflicts between parents and children, especially during the teen years, but families can still be kind to one another. Oftentimes, these conflicts are personality related. Regardless of the personalities involved, it is important to learn to develop a positive relationship with your loved ones.

If you have a basic understanding of the personalities, you can better communicate with one another. There are personalities that thrive on conflict. When you understand this, you can learn how to deal with them without feeling you are being threatened and manipulated. Other personalities need constant encouragement and wilt under harsh criticism.

As a parent, when you understand what your child's personality is, then you can work to tailor his or her discipline and instruction to meet those needs. Proverbs tells us to "train up a child in the way he should go"; the original Greek says in the "bend or bent he should go." God has designed your child with a particular bend or bent and when you understand what it is, getting along is easier for everyone involved!

My youngest daughter was taking piano lessons from a highly recommended instructor. The teacher would tell me how well Sharon was doing, but she wouldn't tell Sharon. Sharon became very discouraged and eventually quit taking lessons from her because she never felt she was meeting her expectations. She was not receiving the positive feedback and encouragement she needed.

Learn how to compliment your children's best efforts even though they may not meet your expectations. Give them space to learn. That means they'll make mistakes and it won't look as good as if you did the work, but they must be able to make mistakes as they learn.

As parents, we need to inspire our children to achieve! We need to give them words of affirmation and bless them. We need to encourage them to pursue their dreams and be all they can be in Jesus. We need to let our words be silver boxes! When our children get involved in things or relationships that are not good for them, we need to remind them that they have a higher calling. Remind them that Jesus has wonderful plans for their lives and that He will always be with them. Remind them of how special they are and that you love them. Encourage them to be leaders and not followers. Let them know it is okay to have a higher standard in their life.

In our society, when we think of giving gifts, we think of giving money or expensive presents, but the gift of encouragement is one of the greatest gifts you can give anyone.

You can give a special gift to every person you meet! You can be the daily source of joy in someone's life simply by the positive words that you say to them!

Ralph Waldo Emerson said, "Rings and jewels are not gifts, but apologies for gifts. The only gift is a portion of thyself."

When you look at the "turning points" of your own life, they rarely involve material goods. Most turning points in life hinge on the positives or negatives you receive from those you love.

Every time we open our mouths, we have a choice to make as to whether we will encourage, uplift, and give hope, or whether we will discourage, put down, and destroy someone by what we say.

The Bible tells us in Proverbs 25:11 "A word fitly spoken is like apples of gold in pictures of silver." I've been told that this was actually the highest award for particular feats that were accomplished. It was a prized and cherished honor to receive apples of gold in pictures of silver.

A kind word, fitly spoken, that brings the priceless gift of encouragement to a person today will be rewarded in time to come, as promised to us by Matthew 6:20 "But lay up for yourselves treasures in heaven, where neither moth nor rust doth corrupt, and where thieves do not break through nor steal."

Apples of gold in shining silver,
That's what our words should be;
May the glowing of Your Spirit
Reflect, O Lord, in me.

Help me to guard each word I speak;
May only love proceed,
So that what others hear from me, Lord,
Is really what they need.
May all my words be seasoned, Lord,
So richly by Thy grace,
That when others look upon me
They see Your glorious face.

> Written by:
> Betty Huizenga
> *Apples of Gold*
> Cook Communications Ministries
> Colorado Springs, CO

The Greatest Gifts a Parent Can Give

CHAPTER FOUR

The Greatest Gifts a Parent Can Give

*J*n this chapter I would like to share my heart with you, though I do want to warn you: Don't turn me off at the beginning of the chapter! If you hang on, I think I can help you to become a better parent and a better child!

This past fall, my grandson was at our house the day the JC Penney Christmas catalog arrived. It didn't take long for John Avery to find the page with all the miniature riding vehicles: cars, motorcycles, and tractors. After a couple of minutes, he said, "Nana Joanne, I need you to buy me all the things on this page!"

As parents and grandparents, I think most of us do try to buy our children what they need or think they need. But being a parent is certainly more than just providing a child with things he wants. Parents have the responsibility to raise a child who will ultimately meet his or her Creator in eternity.

Train up a child in the way he should go: and when he is old, he will not depart from it. (Proverbs 22:6)

It is an awesome responsibility and not an easy task. Dr. James Dobson wrote a book entitled *Parenting Isn't for Cowards.* How true!

I know my children haven't been perfect and we haven't been perfect parents, but I thank the Lord for helping us to raise them in the fear and admonition of Him. I think He has given us some key guidelines to do this that I would like to share with you.

There are three things I would like to share with you in your role as a parent and one thing I would like to share with you in your role as a child, and remember you are still someone's child!

In your role as a parent, I want to encourage you to do these three things:

- Be a mean mom or dad,
- Let your children fail
- And don't be your child's friend!

In your role as a child, I want to encourage you to do this:

- Honor thy father and thy mother.

Now that I have given you a moment to catch your breath, remember I said: Don't turn me off! Let me explain!

As a parent—First: Be a mean mom or dad.

Several years ago, this little vignette was in our local newspaper:

Mean Mothers

Was your Mom mean? I know mine was. We had the meanest mother in the world! While other kids ate candy for breakfast, we had to have cereal, or eggs, or toast. When others had a Pepsi and a Twinkie for lunch, we had to eat sandwiches. And as you can guess our mother fixed us a dinner that was different from what other kids had, too, and she made us all eat together as a family.

Mother insisted on knowing where we were at all times. You'd think we were convicts in a prison. She had to know who our friends were, and what we were doing with them. She insisted that if we said we would be gone for an hour, we would be gone for an hour or less.

We were ashamed to admit it, but she had the nerve to break the Child Labor Laws by making us work. We had to wash the dishes, make our beds, clean our rooms, learn to cook, vacuum the floor, do laundry, and all sorts of cruel jobs. I think she would lie awake at night thinking of more things for us to do.

She always insisted on us telling the truth, the whole truth, and nothing but the truth. By the time we were teenagers, she could read our minds. I think she could even see through walls! Then life was really tough!

Mother wouldn't let our friends just honk the horn when they drove up. They had to come up to the door so she could meet them. While everyone else could date when they were twelve or thirteen, we had to wait until we were much older!

Because of our mother, we missed out on lots of things other kids experienced. None of us have ever been caught for shoplifting, vandalizing other's property, or ever arrested for any crime. None of us have ever done drugs, got drunk, or started smoking. It was all her fault!

Now that we have left home, we are all God-fearing, educated, honest adults. We are doing our best to be mean parents just like Mom was. I think that is what's wrong with the world today. It just doesn't have enough mean moms anymore!

Written by Bobbie Pingaro (1967) Abridged version. (See appendix for unabridged version.)

Don't you agree that we need more mean moms and dads who care about what their children do? We need to be parents who hold their children accountable to do the right thing and who take the time and energy to show their children they love them by being a good example for them and setting some parameters in their lives! Kids don't feel their parents really care about them when they don't set boundaries for them and aren't involved in their lives! I hear it and see it every day!

Second: Let them fail.

Do you realize that perhaps one of the best things you could do for your child is to let him fail? As parents we want the very best for our children. We do all we can to set the stage for them to succeed in everything they do.

As a baby, we prop them up with pillows so if they fall they will not be hurt. We buy them every toy and gadget that we feel will stimulate them to develop to their best potential. If they have problems in school we blame the teacher or the "system." We intervene in situations so that our children aren't "hurt" when they make bad decisions, and we make excuses for them.

As a teacher, I see parents who color the child's pictures and do the child's homework so they won't fail, and refuse to allow children to be held back in school, even though they lack the maturity or necessary skills to go to the next level. Parents pay for speeding tickets, get fines "fixed," pay for abortions to protect their child's "future," and lie for them in court.

Parents see their child failing in some aspect of life, so they run to prop them up. The next failure, they prop them up again. Eventually the props are so adequately placed that no one knows there is a problem with immaturity, irresponsibility, and a lack of basic skills, until the rug is literally pulled out from under them and they can't stand on their own two feet.

They can't get their balance and they fall so hard that even Mom and Dad can't fix it any more.

We need to let our children fail in the little things of life so they can learn to make right choices in the big things. They need to learn that there are consequences to their decisions and realize their need to seek counsel of others, especially their parents.

Children need boundaries and they need consequences. Without either of these parameters, children feel they are "free-falling." Kids will test your limits, but for the most part, they will choose to remain within those bonds of security.

The prodigal son demanded that his father give him his share of the birthright early. With such an important decision, I am sure the father gave him wise counsel, or at least tried to. The father could have refused to let the young man have his inheritance, but he did not seek to control every aspect of his life. He allowed his son to go his own way, to make his own decision.

The father never followed his son to protect him. He wasn't there to bail him out of the pigpen. He simply waited for him to humble himself, come to his right mind, and come home. He let him fail.

Throughout the ages, men and women have had to make choices. When they were good they reaped the benefits; when they were bad they reaped the consequences.

We must give our children the chance to choose and allow them to fail in the little things so they will be able to seek advice and make appropriate choices in the big things and not fail.

I remember a situation with my oldest daughter. She was just getting to the age where Play-Doh was too immature for her. She had some money to spend on something for herself, so we went shopping. She wanted to buy the Play-Doh set that squished the dough out the plastic person's head, for hair. I wasn't real keen on the potential mess but I didn't address that issue with her. I just mentioned that long-term, I thought she might like something else. I gave her the opportunity to make the final decision, and she went for the Play-Doh set. When she got home and opened it, she immediately regretted making the decision. The next time we went to the store, she returned it and purchased something else. I noticed that the next time a decision was to be made, she immediately sought Mom's advice!

Third: Don't be their friend.

My oldest daughter is the "classic" strong-willed child. One day, as a teenager, she became so angry with me that she yelled, "You're not my friend!" I really felt the Lord spoke through me as I responded very calmly with, "You're right, Amy; I'm not your friend. I'm your mother. Maybe one day we can be friends, but right now I'm your mother."

Too many parents cower at those types of outbursts. They want to be their child's friend. They so much want their children to love them that they cave in to their demands, much to the detriment of their children. You must be the parent. You must be the one in charge.

Parents are so busy today that they try to do whatever they can to appease their children, thinking that it is the easier route. It may seem so at first, but it will lead to overwhelming problems that you can't even imagine!

Today, Amy would tell you I am her best friend! But I guarantee you, had I given in to her strong will, she would not be saved today!

In your role as a child:

(Remember, I said we are all children.)

Exodus 20:12 commands us to "Honour thy father and thy mother." And Ephesians 6:1-3 instructs us: "Children, obey your parents in the Lord: for this is right. Honour thy father and mother; (which is the first commandment with promise;) that it may be well with thee, and thou mayest live long on the earth."

God has given order to the family. I think most of us understand that. The husband/father is to be the head of the home, submitting himself to the will of the heavenly Father. The wife is to be subject to her husband, not as his doormat but as his helpmeet, and the children are to submit themselves to their parents and, in doing so, will be blessed of the Lord.

The Ten Commandments which were given to Moses to govern Israel, God's chosen people, are still in effect today.

I don't know if you have ever heard of Dr. Laura Schlessinger, but she is a very conservative radio talk show host who is Jewish. She knows the law—the Jewish law—and she does not pull any punches when people call her for answers to questions in their lives. If someone calls to ask for advice and tells her she is "living with her fiancé," she responds with, "Oh, you mean you're shacking up?"

I once heard her explaining the significance of the Ten Commandments. She said that God had a very specific plan when He wrote the commandments, even as to the order in which they were given. She said that the fifth commandment

(Exodus 20:12 and Deuteronomy 5:16) is pivotal because it divides the commandments related to God from those related to our fellowman. Schlessinger said that when families are out of step in the home, when children aren't honoring their mother and father as the Scriptures decree, they will be out of step with God and with their fellow human beings. This is key—think about it: In the parental relationship we learn first how to submit to the Lord and then how we are to serve our fellowman!

> *Honour thy father and thy mother, as the LORD thy God hath commanded thee; that thy days may be prolonged, and that it may go well with thee, in the land which the LORD thy God giveth thee.* (Deuteronomy 5:16)

Stop to think about that for a minute. If we are not in right relationship with our parents, honoring and respecting them, how can we truly honor and respect the Lord or ever hope to relate well to our fellowman?

People often relate to God as they related to their father. If they had a loving and kind father, that is how they view God; if their father was cruel, they think God is cruel and that He lays traps for them just to see them destroyed.

Now let me interject something here: You may not have had good parents. You may have come from a very dysfunctional family. Your parents may have hurt you deeply. It's a fact, not all parents are good; some are just plain evil. But you are still commanded to honor them because of their position. That means, you forgive them, you harbor no evil against them, and you go on with your life. That doesn't mean that you set yourself up to continually be hurt by them. God does not require that of you. Hopefully, as a result of your experience, you have determined to be a better parent to your own children and to break the cycle of abuse which you were subjected.

Teens often have a difficult time holding their parents in high respect. What they need to realize is that parents are not just two old fools out to ruin their lives. Parents are placed in our lives by the sovereign will of the almighty God to be our overseers until we reach maturity. They're not perfect; they are going to make mistakes. There are still times when my kids roll their eyes and say, "that's just Mom," but they respect me, love me and appreciate everything I have done for them.

It is amazing that as you get older, you find that your parents aren't as dumb as you may have thought they were! Mark Twain once said, "When I was fourteen years old, my father was so ignorant I hated to have the old man around. But when I was twenty-one years old, I was astonished to see how much my father had learned in only seven years!"

Several years ago, when my son was a teen, we had a family visit us with their very unruly children. They wouldn't listen to their parent's instructions, they were destructive, and they would walk around with messy food in their hands, wiping their food and mouths across the furniture and even on the steps. If you told them to stop doing something they would continue doing it with a vengeance. The parents literally had no control of these four children under ten years old. John David came into our room one night and laid across the bed to talk with us. Over and over he thanked my husband and me for disciplining him as a child. He just couldn't believe that children could be so unmanageable, and he was thankful that his parents had raised him with discipline and manners.

Dennis Rainey, a Christian family counselor, recently told a story about his daughter who went through a very rebellious time when she was a teenager. She wanted to know why she had all these rules. She demanded to know why she couldn't be free to express herself and do what she wanted to do.

During this time, the family went on a vacation. They had some friends watch their beloved pet bird. While they were gone, the bird, who liked to get out of its cage, ended up actually flying out of the house! His daughter was devastated because it was her favorite pet. Rainey asked his daughter why the bird needed to be kept in a cage. He asked her what was wrong with just letting the bird fly where it wanted and do what it wanted. She told him that the cage was for the bird's protection. What a teachable moment the Lord afforded Rainey as he proceeded to talk to his daughter, "Yes, you want to protect him, so you keep him in a cage. That's exactly why we have rules for you. We want to protect you!" She understood the message loud and clear! (In case you're wondering, fortunately for her, the bird did come back. What an awesome God we have!)

The gifts I've shared with you in this chapter bring the

promise of a fruitful, enjoyable life in your family relationships as well as with the Lord Jesus Christ!

- Be a mean mom,
- Let your children fail,
- Don't be your child's friend!
- Honor thy father and thy mother.

Take time right now to ask Jesus to guide you in your relationships with your loved ones. Everything in our society is trying to tear the family apart. Now, more than ever, we need His divine hand of mercy to guide us through this life.

The Power of Your Shadow

CHAPTER FIVE

The Power of Your Shadow

One day, while sitting in a restaurant in Toronto, I noticed a lone flower in a vase on a brick column across the room. The flower was about fifteen inches high, but the lights that were shining on it made it cast a shadow almost the entire length of the brick column.

That is when the Lord spoke this thought into my heart:

"We, as individuals, truly are nothing in the scheme of time and eternity, no more than a solitary flower sitting in a vase, but the shadow we cast, be it for good or for evil, far exceeds who we really are!"

The Lord spoke to me about the power of our shadow and that as women, though we may think we are insignificant, our shadow has a tremendous influence on others. You may not think that your influence is all that noticed or important, but people are watching you. Your testimony, be it good or bad, is a shadow that often precedes you and always follows you!

The Book of Acts tells us that after Jesus left the earth, people sought out His disciples, the followers of Jesus. Acts 5:15 says that people lined the streets where Peter was expected to walk, in the hopes that his shadow would pass over them and they would be healed. If you are a disciple of Jesus, others should want your shadow to touch them, too!

Colossians 3:2 tells us to "Set your affection on things above, not on things on the earth."

When we set our affection on things above and endeavor to live our life so we can go there, we are maturing in Christ. Reverend Darrel Johns shared this thought at a marriage retreat, and it really caught my attention. He said that as we mature in Christ, relationships become more and more important to us. Why do you think that is?

As we mature spiritually, we realize that the only thing we will take with us to heaven, to the "above" as mentioned in Colossians 3:2, is people.

In Job 1:21 Job said, "Naked came I out of my mother's womb, and naked shall I return thither."

And it's true, there is no thing on this earth that we can take with us when we die or when we are raptured. But we can take other people with us. It's all that really matters!

And how do we do that? By living our life here on earth so that we affect others and win them to Christ. We win others to Christ by our witness, or our influence on them. By our shadow.

So then comes the question, how do I live my life so I can

influence people and win them to Christ? How can I best cast my shadow?

We do this by doing what the Lord requires of us.

He hath shewed thee, O man [mankind], what is good; and what doth the LORD require of thee, but to do justly, and to love mercy, and to walk humbly with thy God? (Micah 6:8)

I feel that this is what the Lord is telling us today: To truly set our affections on things above, we need to do what He requires of us here:

- To do justly
- To love mercy
- And to walk humbly with our God

In doing so, we will influence others to "set their affections" on things above.

So how do we "do justly, love mercy, and walk humbly with our God"? We do these things by obeying the Scriptures that pertain to us specifically as women.

To do justly—means we must be honest and live honorably or rightly.

Let's take a look at Titus 2:

But speak thou the things which become sound doctrine: That the aged men be sober, grave, temperate, sound in faith, in charity, in patience. The aged women likewise, that they be in behaviour as becometh holiness, not false accusers, not given to much wine, teachers of good things; that they may teach the young women to be sober, to love their husbands, to love their children, to be discreet, chaste, keepers at home, good, obedient to their own husbands, that the word of God be not blasphemed. (Titus 2:1-5)

These Scriptures are not just for married women; they are for all women. Remember, we are all the bride of Christ whether we have an earthly husband or not!

Titus has much to say to us:

- The word "sober" means to have a sound mind. God wants His ladies to have a sound mind.
- We are not to be false accusers or talebearers. We are not to play "telephone" with gossip as we pass it to others.
- To be discreet means to be self-controlled, to be temperate, to watch our temper and to control our tongue from foul language, outbursts of anger, and gossip. Discreet also means to be a good manager of what you have, taking care of what you have and spending your resources wisely by living within your means financially.
- To be chaste means to be modest, not drawing attention to yourself or bragging about yourself. It also means to be clean: both inwardly and outwardly. It means to be pure and innocent. I think it means to stay away from

chat rooms, soap operas, movies, magazines, and books that fill our minds with the filth of the world. Do you remember the story of Pandora's box? To many, the Internet is their Pandora's box. Because of curiosity, they open themselves up to unbelievable temptations, thinking they are capable of handling the enticement—only to find themselves in the jaws of the enemy!

- To be "keepers at home" means to be domestically inclined. It doesn't mean that you have to be a stay-at-home mom. I personally have worked outside the home for thirty years of our thirty-four years of marriage to help support our family, just as many of you do. Being a "keeper at home" doesn't mean that you do all the housework, but it does mean that you care for your family, that you make sure that your home is clean and that your family is properly fed nutritionally balanced meals. To do all of this means that you will have to be organized. You cannot be lazy and accomplish all that the Lord would have you to do.

- Proverbs 31:11-12 "The heart of her husband doth safely trust in her, so that he shall have no need of spoil. She will do him good and not evil all the days of her life." You do your husband "good" by living within your means. You do him good by respecting him and by not putting him in a position to be embarrassed by your actions. You do your husband good by honoring him and speaking highly of him to others, especially your children.

- To be obedient to her own husband. Yes, that means submission!
- You do Jesus good by honoring Him and speaking highly of Him to others, as well as by being submissive to Him!

And why is all this so important? Let's look again at the last part of Titus 2:5 "that the word of God be not blasphemed."

The second thing we need to do is to love mercy.

Boy, this can be a hard one!

- This means that we live a life of kindness,
- we rarely reprove others,
- we are quick to forgive.

I personally believe that unforgiveness is one of the biggest problems within the church today.

Have you ever noticed that none of us ever feel we are one of Joseph's brothers? We all feel we are Joseph, the victim, yet surely we have offended others.

People get offended and don't do what the Bible says to do, which is to go to that person and tell him he has offended them. That's the only way things can truly be worked out. I would venture to say that most offenses weren't done intentionally and that the person who did the offending is not even aware that the person is offended.

How can we really say we love mercy when we can't forgive people?

Jesus said in Luke 17:1-4 "Then said he unto the disciples, It is impossible but that offences will come: . . . Take heed to yourselves: If thy brother trespass against thee, rebuke him; and if he repent, forgive him. And if he trespass against thee seven times in a day, and seven times in a day turn again to thee, saying, I repent; thou shalt forgive him."

In this life, we just need to face the fact that we will be offended. We will be hurt. We will question why people treat us the way they do. But the ultimate question is: how will we respond?

Will we respond with mercy?

Will we respond with forgiveness?

Do you realize that Jesus uses offenses like we use sandpaper?

He wants to smooth the rough edges in our life, and He does it abrasively at times.

I'll never forget the day I was reading my Bible and I realized that when John the Baptist was in prison, he became offended at Jesus. There he was sitting in prison because he preached about Jesus, and Jesus was free to continue teaching. He couldn't go to Jesus in person, so he sent word to Jesus, "Are you the Christ or do we look for another?" When he heard Jesus' response, he never questioned Him again. Obviously he forgave Jesus.

Jesus taught us the ultimate forgiveness when in the midst of His crucifixion, He called out from the cross, "Father, forgive them; for they know not what they do."

And the third thing we need to do is:

To walk humbly with our God.

A note in the margin of my Bible about this part of Micah 6:8 says that in the Hebrew, this passage correctly interpreted means to humble thyself to walk with your God. We must humble ourselves.

How do we "humble ourselves"? By not thinking more highly of ourselves than we ought to. We humble ourselves by not trying to set ourselves up in some position but allowing God to raise us up. We humble ourselves by being servants to God and to others and not expecting others to serve us.

We humble ourselves by being different from the world. God requires us to be set apart, sanctified for Him. The Scriptures say that we are a chosen generation, a peculiar people. We are to look different and act different from the world.

It's difficult for some people to live for God today because they don't want to be different! They say they are their own people and can do what they want, yet they flock to purchase brand-name clothing so they will look like everyone else! You wouldn't believe how many girls are literally wearing their flannel pajama bottoms to school because it is currently the "in thing"! And young men wear their pants low on their hips so their underwear is exposed!

Walking humbly with God doesn't mean that you wear ragged clothes and that you walk around looking downcast all the time. When we first went to Germany, the ladies in our church wore bobby socks and tennis shoes to church and they pinned tears in their clothing with the pins on the outside so they would look humble. My Bible says that God's women are clothed with scarlet, tapestry, silk, and purple, the finest fabrics kings can buy! (Just try to get them on sale!)

To live for God and walk with Him, we will have to humble ourselves and be willing to be different, regardless of what others might think of us or say about us.

Sometimes people say things about you just to see what you are really made of. They may mock you. They may call you a lunatic like they did Jesus Himself. Jesus warned us this would happen.

> *Blessed are ye, when men shall revile you, and persecute you, and shall say all manner of evil against you falsely, for my sake.* (Matthew 5:11)

Now I ask you: How is your shadow of influence doing?

Are you living your life in such a way that you are drawing others to Christ?

Are you trying your best to do all that God requires of you?

Are you doing justly?

Are you honest in your dealings?

Are you living an honorable life, or are you seeking after a relationship with someone that you know is not right?

Is your speech what it should be? Do you have trouble keeping your tongue from cursing or gossip?

Are you one in whom Jesus can trust?

Do you love mercy?

Are you truly kind to people?

Are you walking humbly with your God, or are you fighting against things of which He has convicted you?

Are you easily offended and find it difficult to forgive?

Are you a servant to God and to others?

Lord, help us project a shadow that is pleasing in Your sight. Help us to do justly, to love mercy, to walk humbly with You, and to have a shadow that draws people to You.

Guard Your Heart

CHAPTER SIX

Guard Your Heart

*Keep and guard your heart with all vigilance and above
all that you guard, for out of it flow the springs of life.*
(Proverbs 4:23, Amplified)

*W*hen you guard something, you watch over it, protect it,
and defend it from being destroyed. I want to encourage
you to guard your heart.

In our culture, the heart is considered to be the center of our
emotions. It is our innermost thoughts and feelings. It is our personality. It is, in essence, who we are.

As mortal beings who are bombarded daily by temptations
designed by Satan to draw us away from God, if we do not guard
our heart, we will fall prey to his devices.

*Wherefore let him that thinketh he standeth take heed
lest he fall. There hath no temptation taken you but such as
is common to man: but God is faithful, who will not suffer
you to be tempted above that ye are able; but will with the*

*temptation also make a way to escape, that ye may be able
to bear it.* (I Corinthians 10:12-13)

I believe that oftentimes our way of escape is predetermined
because we have already decided in our heart what we will do if we
are ever in a particular situation.

Each of us must establish in our heart and mind a line that
we will not cross. We must know clearly what rules of conduct
or personal standards to which we will adhere. Once the guidelines are established, it is easier to live by them. When temptations come, you rehearse what you have already established in
your heart. You remind yourself that in your life, it is not an
issue. You won't even allow your mind to consider the thought
because you are not tempted by it.

*So shall they fear the name of the LORD from the west,
and his glory from the rising of the sun. When the enemy
shall come in like a flood, the Spirit of the LORD shall lift up
a standard against him.* (Isaiah 59:19)

We don't have to be overtaken by the flood of the enemy's
temptation when the standard is established in our life.

A missionary's wife once told me of an incident she encountered in a foreign land. She stopped for coffee one morning at an
outdoor café, and before she knew it, a man stopped by her table
and invited her to his apartment. She was totally surprised to find
herself being propositioned, but she had no trouble telling him in

no uncertain terms that she was not interested.

She had established in her heart that she would never even entertain those thoughts. She politely turned the man down, but it made her realize that regardless of her age and her extra pounds, she could have been very vulnerable had she not set up a standard in her heart.

Our culture has many temptations that have entrenched society and broken down fundamental principles.

- Stress, caused by people who are too committed in their time, tempts people to lie, and cheat.
- Stress, caused by people who are over their head in debt, tempts people to cheat, lie, and steal.
- Offenses that are not resolved lead to bitterness and unforgiveness and tempt people to seek revenge rather than allowing God to fight their battle for them and help them to forgive.
- When people don't feel their needs are being met, they become vulnerable in relationships, and they open themselves up to adulterous relationships.
- The Internet can captivate the minds of people and lure them into things in which they never imagined they would become involved. Chat rooms have destroyed hundreds, perhaps thousands of marriages, even in the church. It has opened the door for innocent children to be exposed to pornography. Some have even been molested and murdered as a result of its luring effect. It isn't called the

"net" or the "web" for nothing. Raise up a standard in your life that keeps you from falling prey to its captivating forces.

I admonish you to guard your heart.

That each one of you should know how to possess [control, manage] his own body (in purity, separated from things profane, and) in consecration and honor, Not [to be used] in the passion of lust, like the heathen who are ignorant of the true God and have no knowledge of His will (I Thessalonians 4:4-5, Amplified).

Establish in your heart a line you will not cross. Determine in your heart the thoughts that you will not entertain and the things you will not do. In doing so, you will be "taking the shield of faith, wherewith ye shall be able to quench all the fiery darts of the wicked."

Watch and pray!

You are the watchman on the wall!

You are the gatekeeper!

Guard your heart!

Ripples of Life

CHAPTER SEVEN

Ripples of Life

If you've ever dropped a stone into a pool of calm water, you know that the surface is quickly covered with widening concentric circles. As the stone breaks the surface of the water, it produces a ripple of waves. The energy of one wave is transferred to the neighboring particles and causes yet another wave. On and on they go. If it's a small pond, the ripples will continue until they reach the shore on all sides.

Just as one small stone can affect the entire surface of a body of water, so can one "small sin" affect a person's entire future and those whose lives are all about them.

"I'm only hurting myself. What I do doesn't affect anyone else." How often have we heard these lines or perhaps said or thought the same things ourselves? This has to be one of Satan's biggest lies.

What we do does affect others!

The old saying, "no man is an island," is still true today. Just as dominoes placed end on end fall, each one touching the next, then the next, so do our lives touch the lives of others, regardless of our position or situation in life. Not only do we touch our immediate family and extended family, but friends and acquaintances are touched as well. Even those we don't know directly, those who "know of us," are touched.

Unfortunately, negative news usually travels faster and farther than positive news, and it is often grossly distorted as it widens with the ensuing ripples.

It is so important to live our lives in such a way that Jesus is truly glorified, a life that will bring glory and honor to our Lord, a life that will cause the "ripples" to bring forth love, joy, and peace, as well as all the other attributes of His Spirit.

Reputations and lives are ruined by sin, even by the very appearance of evil!

If you fall into sin, you may one day regain your place in God's kingdom through sincere repentance, but what of those whose lives have been devastated by your actions? What will become of them? For what will you be held accountable?

Let us ever be aware of the effect of our actions as we make ripples in our lives. A life lived as a testimony for Jesus Christ has waves that touch eternity.

Well Diggers and Wall Builders

CHAPTER EIGHT

Well Diggers and Wall Builders

*T*here he stood; she couldn't believe her eyes! It was the same young man whom she had seen before, not in real life but rather in a vision.

Catherine Chambers remembered the experience vividly. One day while standing by her kitchen sink, an overwhelming compulsion came over her to pray. She immediately went to her knees and began to pray earnestly in intercession. In the midst of her prayer, God gave her a vision of a young man. He was imprisoned in a bamboo cage somewhere in the steamy jungles of Southeast Asia. A prisoner of war! She saw immediately his desperate physical, mental, and spiritual needs, and she prayed fervently for him. Finally the burden lifted and she went on with her work.

Little did she realize that she would ever see him again, yet there he stood. She went to the young man to ask if he had been a prisoner of war and he testified indeed of his desperate situation, describing exactly the scene that she had observed in her vision. He then went on to tell of his miraculous deliverance. He was a living testimony of the power of intercessory prayer.

What Catherine Chambers had done was dig a well for a young man who was unable to dig his own well. Prayer digs wells for others so that in their drought they can have waters of refreshing, waters of deliverance, healing, and salvation.

In Deuteronomy 6:11, God said that the children of Israel would draw water from wells that they did not dig. Someone had to go before them to dig the wells so that they could receive the waters of refreshment and nourishment, and so it is with prayer. There are days or periods of time in each of our lives when we don't have the strength physically or spiritually to pray for ourselves. We are in a spiritual drought and need someone else to pray for us, someone else to dig a well for us.

Look around you. There are people everywhere who need your prayers. New converts need your prayers because, for the most part, they don't know how to pray for themselves. Young people need prayer. They face unbelievable pressures from their peers and the culture. Your pastor and assistant pastor need prayer. Just look around your congregation. There are untold needs for which to pray, let alone your own family, friends, and acquaintances.

Not only does prayer dig wells, but it also builds walls of protection. Missionaries need our prayers as they battle spiritual wickedness and darkness in foreign lands. We all need protection as we fight the powers of spiritual darkness in our own home-towns. As our children go to school each day, we need to pray a wall of protection around them.

Well Diggers and Wall Builders

One thing that is so beautiful about our prayer life is that as we intercede for others, we grow in faith ourselves. We dig wells for our own spiritual refreshing and build walls of protection about ourselves.

Let us dig wells and build walls together as we unite spiritually, daily, in prayer, asking God to intercede for the needs of others as we remain their secret prayer partners.

Informed Intercessor

CHAPTER NINE

Informed Intercessor

*T*o pray effectively, you need to be an informed intercessor. To be informed means to have knowledge, to have information. An intercessor is a go-between, one who prays for another person and pleads in behalf of another.

God wants us to be informed intercessors. Thetus Tenney says prayer should be like focused light. She uses the example of the power of a flashlight to dispel the darkness in a pitch-dark room. Modern science has harnessed focused light in lasers. Today, surgery can actually be accomplished by appropriating focused light.

We need to learn how to focus our prayers so they are powerful weapons as they are intended to be. Generic medicine may work just as well as the brand-name stuff, but generic prayers are very weak. Focused prayer versus generic prayer is like comparing the effect of a 60-watt light bulb to a laser beam. There is no comparison!

We also need to learn the value and power of praying in the Holy Spirit. We know that when we receive the baptism of the

Holy Spirit that we speak in tongues, but the Holy Spirit is more than a onetime speaking in tongues experience.

It is vitally important that we speak in tongues. Speaking in tongues is a sign that follows those who believe in Jesus as Savior and Lord.

And these signs shall follow them that believe; In my name shall they cast out devils; they shall speak with new tongues. (Mark 16:17)

When you speak in tongues, you are actually praying. Praying in tongues strengthens your spirit. It builds your holy faith.

He that speaketh in an unknown tongue edifieth himself; but he that prophesieth edifieth the church. (I Corinthians 14:4)

The word "edified" means to charge (like to charge a battery). Eating healthy food strengthens or charges the human body. Praying in your heavenly language, or speaking in tongues, strengthens your spirit.

When you pray in tongues, your spiritual enemy cannot understand and easily oppose your prayer.

For he that speaketh in an unknown tongue speaketh not unto men, but unto God: for no man understandeth him; howbeit in the spirit he speaketh mysteries. (I Corinthians 14:2)

Speaking in tongues allows you to pray strategically. In any type of sport, the opposing team is never told the game strategy. If the other team knew every move that was to be made, it would be fruitless to play the game. Dealing with the enemy of your soul is not a game, but rather spiritual warfare. The enemy of your soul makes constant strategic moves against your spirit when you speak in a "known tongue." But when you pray in an unknown tongue, it is more difficult for the enemy to directly oppose those prayers.

Praying in tongues allows you to intercede according to the perfect will of God. It adds power to your prayer as it aligns your prayer with God's will.

Likewise the Spirit also helpeth our infirmities: for we know not what we should pray for as we ought: but the Spirit itself maketh intercession for us with groanings which cannot be uttered. And he that searcheth the hearts knoweth what is the mind of the Spirit, because he maketh intercession for the saints according to the will of God. And we know that all things work together for good to them that love God, to them who are the called according to his purpose. (Romans 8:26-28)

Praying in tongues increases the effectiveness of prayer for others (Romans 8:27). Prayers that are limited to your natural understanding can also limit God.

For if I pray in an unknown tongue, my spirit prayeth, but my understanding is unfruitful. What is it then? I will pray with the spirit, and I will pray with the understanding also: I will sing with the spirit, and I will sing with the understanding also. (I Corinthians 14:14-15)

Sometimes our own inability to understand what God may be doing in a situation can cause us to be off target in our prayers. Praying in your heavenly language allows God to make intercession through you so that His will can be accomplished in the earth.

We should pray in the Spirit because the Bible tells us to!

Praying always with all prayer and supplication in the Spirit, and watching thereunto with all perseverance and supplication for all saints. (Ephesians 6:18)

But ye, beloved, building up yourselves on your most holy faith, praying in the Holy Ghost. (Jude 20)

Prayer is one of the most important things we can do. Prayer can actually change the mind of God. In portions of the Bible where it says "God repented," it doesn't mean He did anything sinful to repent over. It actually means that He changed His mind, usually as a result of someone's prayer. Abraham pleaded with God to save Lot, and the Lord gave Lot a way of escape. Moses pleaded with God to save the children of Israel after they worshiped the golden calf they made. Hezekiah was on his deathbed and would have died, but God granted him fifteen more years of life. Unfortunately, when he did die, he was in a backslidden condition. All the more reason to pray in the Spirit for the perfect will of God in every situation.

Praying in the Spirit—praying in tongues—is a gift that the Lord has granted us so that He can truly use us in these last days.

Jesus doesn't need our prayers to do anything, but He covets the relationship that prayer affords as we spend time in His presence.

Praying in the Spirit will allow you to be an informed intercessor as you communicate with God and allow Him to work through you.

Too
Blessed
to Be
Stressed

CHAPTER TEN

Too Blessed to Be Stressed

*I*f I could ask you this question, "Do you ever feel stress?" what would your response be? You're probably thinking, *Do I ever feel stress? That's the understatement of the year!*

I recently taught on stress in our Radiant Life classes, and twenty-one of the twenty-two ladies who attended chose to come to my class! Singles, retirees, mothers of toddlers, and mothers of teens! It doesn't seem to matter what season of life you are in, you feel stress.

We know stress as tension and pressure.

Stress is something that we all experience, especially in these last days. It's a "fact of life." The question is: how can we deal with it and what is the best way to relieve it in our lives? The first thing we need to understand is where the stress is coming from.

What makes us stressed? Many things cause stress in our lives. In this chapter, I would like to help you pinpoint where your stress is coming from and share positive ways to deal with it. Ask the Lord to help you understand where your stress is coming from and how He can help you manage it.

This is a list of some of the major stressors of the day. I'll describe them in more detail as we go on:

- Anger
- Painful emotions—guilt, fear, envy, and jealousy
- Low self-esteem
- Grief
- Job stress
- Financial pressures
- Unmet needs
- Parental pressures
- Unexpected events
- Hormonal changes

We all experience stress and we react to it in one way or another. Stress, also known as tension, is energy. Energy will always strive to be discharged, just like a teapot being heated on the stove. When it gets to the boiling point, it sends out a jet stream of pressure that must escape or it will blow the lid off.

We are all kind of like a teapot. Some people have a very small storage area in their teapot and the lid is never on it tightly. It doesn't take much stress/tension/pressure for them to explode. They immediately discharge their stress no matter whom it hurts, taking out their stress on others. Some would say they have a short fuse.

Others have a very large storage area in their teapot and they rarely open their lid. As stress/tension/pressure builds and builds inside them, it develops into psychosomatic illnesses, depression, avoidance, and procrastination.

To live a balanced life in Christ, we need to know what causes stress in our life and learn appropriate ways to reduce it. I'm sure there are many more stressors than I will cover in this chapter, but I will try to cover the ones with which most of us deal.

Anger causes stress. (I'll bet you didn't know that!) I'm sure you've heard the story about the man whose boss yelled at him at work, who went home and yelled at his wife, who yelled at their child, who kicked the dog who bit the cat. . . . Unfortunately, anger breeds anger.

When you realize you are angry with someone, probably the hardest thing, but definitely the best thing, you can do is take it to the Lord. The next thing you need to do is forgive whoever it is who has hurt you, even if they never ask for forgiveness. God can help you forgive them.

Do you realize that forgiveness is really a gift you give yourself? Forgiveness is releasing a person whom you would really like to harm because of how they have hurt you.

Let's think about Joseph for a minute. Joseph certainly was the victim of a horrible deed and he had every right to hate his brothers. I think it is interesting that by the time he found his brothers, God had given him the power to destroy them with no retribution. No one would have said a word if he would have annihilated them because of what they had done to him. But—by that time—he came to the realization that though they meant it for evil, God had a higher purpose in allowing Joseph to be sold into slavery. And Joseph was man enough to accept that truth—so he chose to forgive his brothers even to the point of having them move in with him so he could support not only them but all of their eleven families!

We need to learn how to control our anger. To have anger is not sin, but how we handle it, how we respond to it, can easily be sin!

> *Be ye angry, and sin not: let not the sun go down upon your wrath.* (Ephesians 4:26)

We have tried to take this literally in our marriage. There were many late nights during our first few years of marriage as we worked through differences of opinions!

We cannot hold on to anger—it makes the stress in our lives build until we can't control it and we end up doing something for which we are very sorry. People who allow anger to build in them do irrational things. We hear of shootings all the time where people just went crazy, and often it stemmed from anger and unforgiveness.

Guilt causes stress. When we have guilt in our lives, we have stress.

We experience peace when we live in a way that supports our values, but when we are living in sin—living a double life—we go against our values and it causes us to feel angry, to be stressed.

When people are living in sin, they project their anger onto those living around them, even going as far as to blame the innocent person for their sin. A person who is having an affair has guilt because that one knows what he or she is doing is wrong, so he or she tries to find inner justification by blaming the innocent spouse for the sin. If you have sin or guilt in your life, you need to take it to the Lord and ask for forgiveness so you can be released from the stress of guilt.

Fear causes stress. When we are fearful, we lash out at people. We even lash out at God. Many things in life cause fear: health issues, financial problems, lies from the enemy. . . .

If we are having problems with finances we lash out at the one who seemingly is wasting money or racking up more debt. We get angry with ourselves when we buy things we don't need, and it becomes an uncontrollable cycle.

If your child runs out in the street and you have repeatedly warned him not to do so, when you finally get a hold on him, you are relieved that he wasn't hurt but you lash out at him because he could have been hurt and didn't heed your warning. Your fear for him, in turn, causes you to be angry with him. It causes stress.

The Scriptures say: "Fear hath torment" (I John 4:18) and: "Casting all your care upon him; for he careth for you" (I Peter 5:7).

Jesus doesn't want us to be a fearful people. Learning how to use the Word of the Lord in prayer and putting our complete trust in the Lord can help us overcome fear. Rebuking the enemy when he tries to bring fear and doubt into your life is another tool to help you overcome fear.

Envy and jealousy both cause stress/tension/pressure. A desire to keep up with the Joneses keeps people from being content with what they have and drives them to the stresses of achieving bigger and better. Envy and jealousy destroy relationships.

Paul said, in Philippians 4:11-12, "Not that I speak in respect of want: for I have learned, in whatsoever state I am, therewith to be content. I know both how to be abased, and I know how to abound: every where and in all things I am instructed both to be full and to be hungry, both to abound and to suffer need."

The Bible says that we are not to compare ourselves to others, and for good reason, because God made us who we are.

> *For we dare not make ourselves of the number, or compare ourselves with some that commend themselves: but they measuring themselves by themselves, and comparing themselves among themselves, are not wise. But we will not boast of things without our measure, but according to the measure of the rule which God hath distributed to us, a measure to reach even unto you.* (II Corinthians 10:12-13)

We need to learn to be content with what we have to relieve stress in our lives. We need to be able to accept where we are in life at the moment, not always struggling to achieve to get more.

Low self-esteem causes stress. Low self-esteem is a major issue in the world today. Worldly people want to look more and more outlandish so they will draw attention to themselves. Somehow they feel that the attention they get will help them to feel better about themselves.

Low self-esteem stems from many sources. Some people have low self-esteem because of situations in their childhood where they were constantly berated and put down and/or physically or sexually abused.

Some have low self-esteem because they always compare themselves to others and they feel they are never as good as other people.

Others with low self-esteem are perfectionists. In order for them to like themselves, they have to be perfect; and since they can't be perfect, they fail their own expectations and it reinforces their low self-esteem. It just becomes a vicious circle!

People with low self-esteem always feel they are the victims. They always feel they are the Joseph, who was wronged, and never the brothers who wronged him!

What we have to realize is that our perception of ourselves, whether it is high or low, is largely formed by what we think others think of us. Let me repeat that: our perception of ourselves is largely formed by what we think others think of us. My brother used to say: I am who I think you think I am.

Research has shown that to be true. Teachers have been given classes of children with below-average ability but were told that the children were significantly above average. The children were perceived to be bright, were taught to that end, and in time their test scores indeed indicated that they were bright!

The children of Israel demonstrated this when ten of the spies returned to Moses with what the Bible calls "an evil report."

And they brought up an evil report of the land which they had searched unto the children of Israel, saying, The land, through which we have gone to search it, is a land that eateth up the inhabitants thereof; and all the people that we saw in it are men of a great stature. And there we saw the giants, the sons of Anak, which come of the giants: and we were in our own sight as grasshoppers, and so we were in their sight. (Numbers 13:32-33)

They saw themselves as grasshoppers, so they figured the giants saw them as grasshoppers too.

As children of God, we need to focus on what God thinks of us! He thought enough of us that He formed us in our mothers' wombs! He thought enough of us that He was willing to die for us on Calvary! Never forget: He says that we are His children, and because He is a king, that makes us royalty!

Jobs cause stress. The actual responsibilities of the job and the personalities with which you deal cause stress, as does the time away from the many other responsibilities of being a wife and mother.

If your job is unbearable, perhaps it's time to look for another job. I still teach school because I enjoy it, but I have been in situations where I haven't always been at a job I liked and I haven't always had a good employment experience. One thing that has worked for me is to pray that God would deliver me from the stressful situation, whether it was the job itself or the people with whom I worked. He can do it!

Unmet needs cause stress. Things we perceive as unmet needs in our lives cause stress, be they emotional needs or physical needs. We live in the most bountiful nation in the world, and if we would carefully look at what we perceive as needs, in relationship to the rest of the world and all of eternity, we would realize that we have very few real physical needs, with the exception perhaps being health issues.

As far as emotional needs: truly only Jesus can meet your emotional needs. Your husband, your parents, your children, or your friends cannot meet your emotional needs. Only Jesus can make you whole and give you true peace.

So many women today jump from one bad relationship to another, thinking that Prince Charming will one day appear. I call this the Cinderella Syndrome. No man is perfect. No man can meet your every need.

When we were in Stockton, I was invited to teach a lesson to the single women in the College and Career class. The Lord gave me a message entitled: A Watched Pot Never Boils! As a single, you can spend your entire life wrapped up in looking for a man to meet your needs, or you can spend your life doing what Jesus has called you to do and allow Him to meet your needs—He just may surprise you!

Parenting pressures—Raising kids isn't easy and it does cause stress. Dr. Dobson wrote a book entitled: *Parenting Isn't for Cowards!* How true that statement is. He also said that when kids turn thirteen they go brain-dead for a few years! Can you relate?

The key to relieving this stress, when raising children, is to be consistent and have follow-through with discipline. Don't make idle threats. I recently had a parent tell me her child was grounded for three years! That is not only unreasonable but it is impossible, and the child knows it.

Another key is that husbands and wives must be on the same page, working toward the same goals and not undermining one another.

Don't try to "buy" your children's affection; they will only learn to expect more and to focus on material things.

Don't try to be your child's friend. (Something I addressed in the chapter "The Greatest Gifts a Parent Can Give.")

Understanding your child's personality helps you to better train them in the way they should go, as the Bible admonishes us to do. ("Treasures of the Heart," a chapter in my book *Growing in All the Right Places*, addresses this issue.)

Then there is the parenting issue on the other end of the spectrum: about the time the childhood/parenting pressures are over, you join the sandwich generation as you begin parenting your parents! Which is another whole set of issues and stressors.

Unexpected events cause stress—a job loss, job transfer, the death of a loved one, long-term illness, retirement. . . . All of these are things that jolt our lives and cause stress. These are situations that eventually most of us will face, at least on this earth. The only answer I have to this is Ecclesiastes 3:1 "To every thing there is a season, and a time to every purpose under the heaven."

Some things we will never understand in this life. The Bible tells us that His ways are past knowing and that now we see through a glass darkly, but there is coming a day when we will know as we are known. That's when we will understand why we have gone through the things through which we have gone.

Hormones cause stress. Modern science has proved that women have hormonal cycles: PMS, peri-menopause, menopause, post-menopause. . . . Again, these stages of life are a "fact of life." One author said that some women use these phases of life to become obsessed with themselves and to provide them with an excuse for inexcusable attitudes and behaviors! This is so very true.

What happens in our bodies does affect us emotionally, mentally, physically, and spiritually, but we fall in the trap of the enemy (Satan) when we justify fleshly, sinful attitudes and responses based on hormonal changes. We cannot allow our emotions to control us.

For thou hast possessed my reins: thou hast covered me in my mother's womb. I will praise thee; for I am fearfully and wonderfully made: marvellous are thy works; and that my soul knoweth right well. My substance was not hid from thee, when I was made in secret, and curiously wrought in the lowest parts of the earth. Thine eyes did see my substance, yet being unperfect; and in thy book all my members were written, which in continuance were fashioned, when as yet there was none of them. How precious also are thy thoughts unto me, O God! how great is the sum of them! (Psalm 139:13-17)

God made us. We are truly designed by the divine! He made us women. He knows how our bodies work and He said that He would never give us more than we can bear! We just need to let Him "possess our reins," as verse 13 says.

Again, I think so much of what we experience is what we perceive we will experience. When I began to go through menopause, I experienced some weird symptoms in my body and I began to feel weird emotionally, so I started to study about the effects of menopause and praying that God would help me to get through the whole thing with the least amount of adversity. I can honestly say that He helped me immensely and it wasn't all that bad!

May God himself, the God of peace, sanctify you through and through. May your whole spirit, soul [including those emotions] and body be kept blameless at the coming of our Lord Jesus Christ. The one who calls you is faithful and he will do it. (I Thessalonians 5:23-24, NIV)

Talk with other women who have been through what you are going through. Talk with your doctor. Talk to Jesus!

There is one more major stressor that I would like to mention. Dr. Kevin Leman wrote a book entitled: *Bonkers: Why Women Get Stressed out and What They Can Do about It.* I was curious to see what he had to say about stress, and it took me until page 184 to find the crux of his message. He said that ultimately the biggest cause of stress in the lives of women today is that they are not organized!

Jean Lush, a Christian family therapist often featured on *Focus on the Family*, in her book: *Women and Stress, a Practical Approach to Managing Tension* said the same thing. She said that when your home is in chaos you become overwhelmed, you don't think straight, you get frustrated, and you give up.

Is this a problem that affects you? If being disorganized is causing you stress, you need to get organized! I know from personal experience that this is much easier said than done. This was a major issue in my life until I found a system that helped me get organized and stay that way. "The Miracle Worker: Organizational Tips for Women," the next chapter in this book, can help you get on top of this stressor and help you stay that way.

Regardless of how you do it, if you need to get your life organized, find a plan and follow it; you will not regret it!

Here is a general list of other things that can help reduce stress in your life:

- Stay ahead of your work. Don't procrastinate. Procrastination compounds stress.
- Do the hard things first.
- Get enough sleep.
- Have a creative diversion. Do something for yourself. This is very important!
- You need some alone time, something you can look forward to, something with which you can reward yourself. As women we forget how to "play." We need to revive that in our lives!

- Take time for yourself. Take time for your husband. Some mothers have to go to the bathroom and lock the door to get a couple of minutes to themselves! I'll never forget a phone call from my youngest daughter about a month after she had her first baby, "Mom, I just can't believe how much time it takes with a baby! I won't be able to sew for the next eighteen years!" There are times when you do feel that way!
- Go shopping (just don't stress your finances!).
- Read the book you've always wanted to read.
- Take a bubble bath.
- Work on a craft you enjoy: paint, knit, scrapbook. . . .
- Attend a fun class at a community college or craft store.
- Take a walk.
- Exercise.
- Write.
- Cry!
- Laugh! Have you have seen the Red Hat Society ladies? I don't belong to a group because I don't have time, but I like the basic principles of their group: no one is allowed to complain about anything the entire time they are at a gathering, and they celebrate their age rather than bemoan it! What stress ladies feel when they are told at forty that they are "over the hill!" "A merry heart doeth good like a medicine" (Proverbs 17:22).
- Learn how to say "No" to taking on more jobs and don't feel guilty.

- Eat properly.
- Take a real vacation, even if it's just for a couple of days.
- Put God back in the picture!

We need to be in relationship with Jesus every day! We were made to know God. He is our source of hope and strength. There is a place in our innermost being that only Jesus can fill. We need to fellowship with Him every day in prayer and by reading His Word. Jesus is the ultimate stress reliever! Jesus said in Matthew 11:28-30, "Come unto me, all ye that labour and are heavy laden, and I will give you rest. Take my yoke upon you, and learn of me; for I am meek and lowly in heart: and ye shall find rest unto your souls. For my yoke is easy, and my burden is light."

When you keep Him first in your life, He will help you understand from where your stress is coming. Is it guilt? Is it envy? Is it not taking proper care of yourself? Is it disorganization?

Perhaps you have never really experienced Jesus living in you. Begin by asking for forgiveness of your sins. Ask Him to fill you with His Spirit.

Jesus doesn't want us to be stressed. He wants us to "work smarter" not "harder"! He wants us to have life and have it more abundantly (John 10:10).

Allow Jesus to help you make the necessary changes to reduce stress in your life.

Are you too stressed to be blessed?
Or are you too blessed to be stressed?

The
Miracle
Worker

(Organizational Tips for Women)

CHAPTER ELEVEN

The Miracle Worker
(Organizational Tips for Women)

*H*ave you ever had unexpected company drop by and been embarrassed because of the way your house looked?

Have you ever had to pay a late fee because you misplaced a bill and didn't pay it on time?

Have you ever looked, seemingly for hours, for something you know you have, you just don't know where it is?

If you have experienced any of these situations, hopefully you will find some help in the pages of this chapter.

I know how you feel. I've been there! Before we were married, I lived with my grandmother. One day my fiancé, now my husband, was at our house doing some work. He told my grandmother that he needed a ruler, so she sent him to my room. After being gone for quite some time, Grandma called upstairs, "John, haven't you found that ruler yet?" His response was, "Ruler? I can't even find her desk!"

Take heart, I'm sure you aren't as bad as some situations I've seen and about which I've heard. My husband and I stopped to visit with a new family who had begun coming to our church.

They warmly greeted us and invited us in. I could scarcely believe my eyes when we walked through the kitchen. It was a total disaster! Not only dirty dishes all over, but the cat was on the counter walking over the dishes and licking the bowls. They ushered us into their living room as they pushed the foot-deep pile of toys and clothes out of the way. Down the hall and around the corner was piled every inch of the way. When we got to the living room, they realized that the cushions were missing on the couch. They had the children run upstairs to see if they could find them. Evidently they had been using them to slide down the steps and had failed to replace them when they were finished. What a mess!

One time a lady came to me wanting help to get her house organized. Her husband had forbidden her to use real dishes. She was relegated to using paper plates all the time because she couldn't seem to get the kitchen clean and the dishes washed between meals.

Phyllis Diller, the wild-haired comedian, must have had trouble with housework, too. She said that she always keeps a desk drawer full of "get well" cards, in case someone dropped over unexpectedly and caught her still in her nightgown at two in the afternoon. She would quickly whip out all the cards and spread them across the mantel. Then when she answered the door, she would feebly say, "Oh, hi. You'll have to excuse the mess. As you can see, I'm just recovering from a really bad bout with the flu!"

One lady said that when she gets company, she puts "out of

order" signs on all the bathrooms except the one that is clean!

There is a better way! I would like to share some things with you that will help you get organized from the inside out. These principles I've gleaned have revolutionized the way I maintain our home, principles that, if followed, will give you more time, peace of mind, and control over the daily, seemingly overwhelming responsibilities of homemakers today. The organizational card file system which I would like to share with you emphasizes a positive attitude, does not expect overnight success, and is achievable.

When we were in Germany, I ran across a book that really ministered to me in this area of my life. I was working full-time, we were pastoring a large, lively church, and I had three small children and a husband to care for. Needless to say, I needed all of the help I could get! I still do! I'm always looking for time-saving tips and hints.

The book was written by two sisters (Pam Young and Peggy Jones) who became absolutely desperate to gain control and organization in their homes. They were known to greet their husbands at the door when they returned from work, still wearing their unchanged nightclothes! One of the marriages actually ended in divorce as a result of an unkempt home, family, and relationship. Through desperation and much prayer, they developed a system to help themselves correct their motives, clean, organize, and maintain their homes efficiently. When they developed and perfected their program, they felt that they should share it with others to help them get out of the mess in which they found themselves. They wrote a book entitled: *S.H.E. Sidetracked Home Executives*, from which the basic plan of this system came from. This book is still available on their Web site *shesintouch.com*, as well as other materials and books designed to help you get organized and stay that way. You may also find this book at your local library or they may be able to order it for you.

There is also a wonderful Web site that incorporates the principles from *S.H.E.* as well as tons of forms, lists, hints, ideas, and encouragement: *flylady.net*.

Before you actually try to begin this plan, I would suggest reading through the next few pages. It will all make more sense to you if you read it to get the big picture. You might also want to check out *flylady.net* before you begin. I do want to caution you to take one step at a time. Don't become overwhelmed and give up before you begin. It is actually easier than it may appear!

To begin this system, you will need the following materials: 3x5 card file box that is extra deep, generic dividers that you can write on, plain white file cards, colored file cards (e.g., yellow, blue, pink), two sets of tabbed A-Z dividers, tabbed 1-31 numbered dividers, blank dividers to label yourself, and a small calendar for the entire year (the size found in your checkbook register is the perfect size). You can find these items at an office supply store for approximately fifteen dollars.

Each card represents a particular sequence of doing chores: yellow for daily chores, blue for weekly tasks, white for monthly and seasonal projects, and pink for personal items and errands. The numbered cards will serve as your tickler file for the days in the month. As a reference, tape the small calendar to the inside of the lid of your box.

One set of alphabetically tabbed index cards will become your address book. Write one name and address on each card as well as pertinent information regarding that person or family. You might want to include birthdays, anniversaries, food preferences, ages of children, sizes, gift ideas. . . . Maintaining this type of address "book" is much more efficient and neater than traditional ones. As people's addresses and information change, simply make a new card for them. You may choose to tape their address label or business card to the card to save some time.

The second set of alphabetical cards is used to file various information. Blank tabbed cards should be labeled with headings such as: Weekly, Home Improvements, Monthly, Projects, Special, Gifts, Mini-jobs, Storage, Twice Yearly, Miscellaneous, Menu Ideas, and other categories you may find appropriate to meet your needs. Remember you are not bound by my suggestions. Each woman has different needs in these areas according to her home and responsibilities.

Take a notebook and pencil and go to each room of your house or apartment. Make a list of every possible job to be done in that room: dust, sweep, mop, wash walls, wash windows, mirrors. . . . Also note the amount of time it would take you to complete each task and how often you do it, or rather should do it! Be realistic in your evaluation. Some things may be done more frequently than we need to, simply because we enjoy it and others not as frequently as we should because it isn't our favorite thing to do. Perhaps it is a chore that should be delegated to someone else. Decide how often it needs to be done: daily, weekly, monthly, semi-annually, or annually. Do this in every room or area of your home. There are free forms available at *flylady.net* to help with this step.

Now transfer each item to the corresponding colored card. Record the job, approximate time involved to complete it and how often to complete it. If it is a job which takes less than ten minutes to complete, then it is considered a mini-job and can be done at odd spare minutes, perhaps while you are talking on the phone or, if the work is portable, such as reading the mail or writing letters, it could be done while you are waiting at the dentist or doctor's office.

One of the most important aspects of this system is to make sure you are up one-half hour before the rest of the mainstream of your family. How you use this time is entirely up to you, but I prefer devotional time. For some totally unknown reason, it seems that everyone else gets up in a better mood when I've had a talk with the Lord first! (Wonder why?)

Another crucial point is having a plan for each day and each week, plus a skeleton plan for the month. You will find if you take time to plan that you will have well-deserved free time to do things that you enjoy doing, plus you will feel so much better about yourself, your family, and the Lord.

At this point you need to make a Basic Week Plan on one of your cards. Write down each day of the week and what your plans are for that day. A good rule of thumb is to plan two days of moderate cleaning, one day of heavy cleaning, one day to run errands and do shopping, one day to be entirely free for yourself, and Saturday and Sunday to be free for church and family. This probably sounds too good to be true, but with desire, discipline, and organization, it is indeed possible!

When you are doing your weekly planning, use your local grocery coupons and plan your week's menus. This will save you time and money. You can purchase everything you need in one trip to the market, which means you don't have to take time to shop later, and it will cut down on the impulse buying. (Statistics show that you save 25 percent or more on your groceries by only going to the grocery store once a week.) I usually plan one trip to our deep discount store per month. I purchase staples and generic items that I know are equivalent to brand-name items for a fraction of the cost.

Now that your mind is all geared up and your file box is ready to go, begin cleaning your house from the inside out! Start at your front door and plan to work clockwise around the house, skipping your kitchen at this point. Put in order every closet, cupboard and drawer in every room until you reach the front door again. (This is the cleaning mentioned in your moderate and heavy cleaning days.) You may not finish an entire room in one week. Don't worry about it; you will get to it eventually.

The key here is to not get sidetracked! Stay in one room until you have finished all of the things that need done in that room. If you are like me, you will probably have to fight the impulse to take something to another room, but this is how you become sidetracked and lose your focus! Again, begin at the front door and work clockwise. As you clean each room, keep your cards handy and make a list of where everything is stored. Another important thing to do is have four boxes or bags going as you clean. This will help you to stay in the room you are working on and not wander from room to room as you put things away. (A huge time-waster!) Label each box or bag:

1. Give away
2. Throw away
3. Put away
4. Storage

If you have not used an item or worn an item of clothing in one year, the chances are very great that you will never use or wear that item again. If you simply can't bear to part with something or it is something that has sentimental value, then put it in storage.

To accomplish your ultimate goal of getting your home clean and organized you need to adopt the theme: Dare to dump it! It's amazing how bold you can be when you keep that thought in mind.

I would caution you, if the stuff you want to dump is not yours, you need to have the owner help in the decision to get rid of the items, or at least give him the opportunity of a deadline to take care of it. Even though you are trying to organize your home, you still need to remember the Golden Rule, to do unto others as you would have them do unto you. I'm sure you wouldn't like for someone else to take it upon himself to throw your things away.

After the main part of your house is clean, then tackle the kitchen. Once again, begin at the main entrance and work your way around the room clockwise. If you don't finish in one day, on the next day you clean, pick up where you left off. After the kitchen, clean your storage area. Put storage items in logical places and keep a record of items in your file-box listing their location. Organizing your storage in this manner will save you hours of time when you need to find something.

The numbered dividers relate to each day of the month. As you make out your weekly plan, put each card behind the date you plan to complete it. Put them in the order you wish to do them in. If you don't complete a task on the assigned day, put it behind the next day, but don't allow this to happen more than three times. If it does, either you don't need to do the job or it is something you don't like to do! Pray about it and ask God to help you get it done!

There are some basic tenets to keep in mind before you begin any type of organizational program; if you don't you are prone to fail because the task will appear overwhelming.

To succeed, keep these thoughts in mind and establish these habits:

- You didn't get into the mess overnight, and you won't get out of the mess overnight!
- When you get up in the morning, get completely dressed, fix your hair, and put on shoes before you begin anything. This will remind you that you have a job to do.

- Never leave the house before you've done all of the everyday duties in the card file box. You will find as you get organized that this will take less and less time.
- Finish what you start. I love to sew, but I will not allow myself to begin anything new until my mending is done.
- Learn to say "no" if you tend to overcommit.
- Make fewer promises, but keep them more faithfully.
- Plan to have a free day; you really need the break and what a satisfying, calorie-free reward!
- Make Christmas lists early and listen for suggestions. (Put suggestions on cards so you don't forget them!) Shopping will be much less hectic and you can save money by picking up things throughout the year when you find them on sale.
- Research shows it takes twenty-one consecutive days to establish a new habit, so be patient with yourself.
- Never leave a room before closing all closets, cupboard doors and drawers.
- Pick it up; don't pass it up!
- When you fix anything to eat, put away everything you used before you sit down to eat.
- You don't need to work harder; you need to work smarter!
- Learn to prioritize! Planning is the key to success. Develop a plan and stick to it. "If you fail to plan, you plan to fail!"
- Women set the tone in the home, whether it is peaceful

and orderly or chaotic! Set the standard for orderliness yourself.

- Don't have an *anytime* routine.
- Put things where they belong when you are through with them.
- Always check the next day's cards the night before. This will help you keep on top of things.
- Do something you enjoy on your free day. Plan a simple meal, eat leftovers, or do carryout that night so you don't have to cook a big meal.

Organizational card file system.

Tools you will need:

- 3" x 5" card file box (If you can find the deeper size, it is better.)
- Small calendar
- 3" x 5" cards: yellow, blue, white, pink
- January-December card guide set
- 1-31 card guide set (one for each day of the week)
- A-Z card guides

The System

Go through your home and make an activity list for every room in the house. Decide how often the job needs done, how long it takes to do the job, and who can do the job. On separate colored cards, write everything you want to accomplish: personal goals, household chores, notes about special occasions, everything you need to remember.

Use the colored 3x5 cards to help you organize the jobs by how often they need to be done. You can use the following colors as examples. The key is to make sure every job gets a card that tells where the job is and how often it needs to be done.

Examples:

Frequency	Color
D = Daily	Yellow
W = Weekly	Blue
EOW = Every Other Week	White
S = Seasonally	White
EOM = Every Other Month	White
2/Y = Twice a year	
M = Monthly	
2/W = Twice a Week	
Personal Notes	Pink

When every job has a card, you file the card on the date in the month when you plan to do that job. Each day you take the cards/jobs out of the file that you need to accomplish that day, and as they are accomplished, you re-file them behind the date when you need to do it next.

- Yellow: job is performed daily or every other day, such as doing the dishes or making the beds. When the task is complete, just re-file the card behind the next date it should be completed.

- Blue: weekly or bi-weekly, such as ironing, changing sheets, or mopping floors.
- White: Monthly or seasonal tasks, such as putting up storm windows or moving seasonal clothes from one location to another. EOM: Every other month.
- Mini-jobs: list jobs that take less than ten minutes on cards. When the phone rings, do one of the jobs as you talk. If it is something portable, such as writing thank you cards or addressing envelopes, take it with you to do as you wait for an appointment.

Have a Basic Week Plan that fits your schedule.

Example:

Monday—	Heavy clean
Tuesday—	Shopping, wash clothes
Wednesday—	Moderate cleaning, iron
Thursday—	Free day
Friday—	Moderate cleaning
Saturday—	Family
Sunday—	Church, family, free of cleaning

Have a Menu Plan (Yellow card)

Sit down with the weekly advertisements and plan a week's worth of meals. (Post the week's menu on your refrigerator for the family to see.) Knowing what you are cooking ahead of time will save you the frustration of trying to cook a frozen hunk of ground beef in a hurry, and it will save you money. Not knowing what to cook leads to more fast-food purchases, and every additional trip to the grocery store adds 25 percent to the cost of weekly groceries. Use your Crock-Pot; it will save you time and money. Make a list of twenty or thirty meals that you normally cook. Write each menu on a card (daily) and as you plan your week, put the meal card behind the date you plan to serve it. The night before, take out the things you need for the next day's meal and make any preparations for which you have time. One day per week, have an extra-special meal. Try some of those recipes you have been cutting out!

Some ladies plan their menus for the entire month and some take one Saturday a month and do all their cooking for the entire month, marking it and freezing it for faster meal preparation later in the month.

Make a master list of all of the meals you make, and keep it in a file of menu ideas. I keep a three-ring binder of recipes I refer to over and over, so I don't have to dig in all of my books to find my favorites. Keep items on hand for a tasty meal you can prepare in a hurry if unexpected company drops by.

Re-file your cards as you complete them.

Establish a plan for cleaning the entire house. Starting at the front door, work clockwise around the house, skipping the kitchen at this point. Clean and put in order each closet, cupboard, and drawer in every room until you reach the front door. Have four boxes or bags with you as you go:

- Give away/sell
- Throw away
- Put away
- Storage

Choose a motivational theme:

- Dare to dump it!
- If in doubt, throw it out!
- Eliminate and concentrate

After the main part of your house is clean, clean the kitchen. Follow the same pattern: start at the main door and work clockwise around the kitchen until you are finished.

Don't "chase rabbits" as you clean! When you find those loose pictures, don't decide that it is time to begin your scrapbooking project. After your cleaning is finished and you develop a routine that allows you the free time to do something you enjoy, make that a project.

After the main part of your house is clean and your kitchen is clean, tackle your storage area. Put storage boxes in logical places. Label your boxes and keep a card file listing the contents of each box.

Establish an office area even if it is just a cardboard box. Have stamps, envelopes, pens, checks, and anything else you need in that area.

Have a strongbox or fireproof box to store: birth certificates, loan papers, passports, guarantees, a copy of your charge cards, marriage license, military papers, school records, Social Security cards and numbers, resumes, job information, letters of recommendation. . . .

Keep a notebook to file home repairs, receipts, and warranties. Keep a record of items you have loaned out: books, tools. . . . You can write the item on a file card and file it in your box for easy reference.

Keep a file for bills to pay. As soon as you receive a bill, file it in the folder. Establish two days a month to pay bills so you remain current. Charge companies are currently charging twenty-nine dollars, plus interest, for late payments!

Use colored file folders to clue you in and save you time in filing.

- Red: bills to pay.
- Blue: receipts of bills paid. (Always write the date and check number on the statement that you retain so you will have a personal record of the transaction.)
- Yellow: mail on hold such as wedding invitations, offers you may be interested in. . . .

Try to handle paperwork once. Open your mail by a trash basket and throw away anything you don't need. Don't save old magazines. Cut out the articles you want and file them. Be careful with any personal information. Identity theft is rampant today. It is a good habit to shred any papers with your name or address on them. In catalogs, I always pull out the order blank that has my name and account information and shred it with the label, usually found on the back cover of the catalog.

Make sure you plan time for Bible study and prayer or there will never be time, no matter how organized you become!

Certainly there is no magical cure for disorganization, but if this plan is implemented, you will be able to maintain your home and have time for yourself and your family.

The Proverbs 31 Lady

CHAPTER TWELVE

The Proverbs 31 Lady

*P*roverbs 31:10-31 in the Amplified Bible reads thus: "A capable, intelligent, and virtuous woman—who is he who can find her? She is far more precious than jewels and her value is far above rubies or pearls. [Proverbs 12:4; 18:22; 19:14.] The heart of her husband trusts in her confidently and relies on and believes in her securely, so that he has no lack of [honest] gain or need of [dishonest] spoil. She comforts, encourages, and does him only good as long as there is life within her. She seeks out wool and flax and works with willing hands [to develop it]. She is like the merchant ships loaded with foodstuffs; she brings her household's food from a far [country]. She rises while it is yet night and gets [spiritual] food for her household and assigns her maids their tasks. [Job 23:12.] She considers a [new] field before she buys or accepts it [expanding prudently and not courting neglect of her present duties by assuming other duties]; with her savings [of time and strength] she plants fruitful vines in her vineyard. [Song of Solomon 8:12.] She girds herself with strength [spiritual, mental, and physical fitness for her God-given task] and makes her arms strong and firm. She tastes and sees that her gain from work [with and for God] is good; her lamp goes not out, but it burns on continually through the night [of trouble, privation, or sorrow, warning away fear, doubt, and distrust]. She lays her hands to the spindle, and her hands hold the distaff. She opens her hand to the poor, yes, she reaches out her filled hands to the needy [whether in body, mind, or spirit]. She fears not the snow for her family, for all her household are doubly clothed in scarlet. [Joshua 2:18, 19; Hebrews 9:19-22.] She makes for herself coverlets, cushions, and rugs of tapestry. Her clothing is of linen, pure and fine, and of purple [such as that of which the clothing of the priests and the hallowed cloths of the temple were made]. [Isaiah 61:10; I Timothy 2:9; Revelation 3:5; 19:8, 14.] Her husband is known in the [city's] gates, when he sits among the elders of the land. [Proverbs 12:4.] She makes fine linen garments and leads others to buy them; she delivers to the merchants girdles [or sashes that free one up for service]. Strength and dignity are her clothing and her position is strong and secure; she rejoices over the future [the latter day or time to come, knowing that she and her family are in readiness for it]! She opens her mouth in skillful and godly Wisdom, and on her tongue is the law of kindness [giving counsel and instruction]. She looks well to how things go in her household, and the bread of idleness (gossip, discontent, and self-pity) she will not eat. [I Timothy 5:14; Titus 2:5.] Her children rise up and call her blessed (happy, fortunate, and to be envied); and her husband boasts of and praises her, [saying], Many daughters have done virtuously, nobly, and well [with the strength of character that is steadfast in goodness], but you excel them all. Charm and grace are deceptive, and beauty is vain [because it is not lasting], but a woman who reverently and worshipfully fears the Lord, she shall be praised! Give her of the fruit of her hands, and let her own works praise her in the gates [of the city]! [Philippians 4:8.]"

Basically, the Proverbs 31 lady
- loves and fears God;
- has her priorities set God's way;
- works hard; is responsible, not idle;
- is considerate of others and their needs;
- looks ahead and prepares for her family's needs;
- takes time to develop her own character;
- is respected and loved by those around her.

As ladies, no two of us are alike. We grew up in different families/environments, currently live in different families/environments, are at different stages of life, and have different daily responsibilities. Some are married, some are single, some are widows, some have empty nests, some have very full nests, but we all serve the same God and have the same responsibilities to Him.

As ye have therefore received Christ Jesus the Lord, so walk ye in him: rooted and built up in him, and stablished in the faith, as ye have been taught, abounding therein with thanksgiving. (Colossians 2:6-7)

If you have received His Spirit, you were born into His Spirit and He wants you to continue to grow in Him.

But seek ye first the kingdom of God, and his righteousness; and all these things shall be added unto you. (Matthew 6:33)

When you seek Him, regardless of what your problems are, He will be there to help you. The key is that you must keep Him first in your life.

The Bible doesn't sugarcoat anything. It is very honest in presenting the lives of people to us. In the Bible we read about many women. We read about their struggles, their trials, their problems, their victories, and their failures.

Esther was married to a heathen king through no choice of her own, but she honored him and respected him. She had great courage as she approached the king to save herself and her entire nation from annihilation.

Sarah was told to pack up everything she owned and to leave her hometown to follow her husband. She had no idea where they were going, but she followed him without question and with the greatest of respect. Later we see that she got impatient with God and decided to take the situation of having an heir into her own hands. We are all suffering with that situation today. The son that Hagar, the bondwoman, bore was the beginning of the religion of Islam!

Miriam, the sister of Moses, tried to put Moses down and usurp authority over him. A bout with leprosy quickly humbled her.

Lot's wife refused to follow Lot as he followed God's instructions, and she was turned into a pillar of salt.

Michal, David's wife, berated him for worshiping God. The Bible says that she was barren and never had any children as a result of that action.

Gomer, the wife of the prophet Hosea, committed adultery and abandoned her husband and her children.

Job's wife should have supported her husband when he faced adversity, but instead she told him to "curse God, and die."

Jezebel was probably the wickedest woman who ever lived. She was so bad that God told the prophet that when she was killed, dogs would eat her carcass, all but her hands and head because they were so wicked.

Hannah wasn't able to have children and was constantly harassed by Peninnah, but she remained faithful to God and to her husband and was longsuffering and prayerful while she waited for the Lord to bless her. Which He gloriously did with the birth of Samuel and then other children.

Huldah, the keeper of the wardrobe, was a prophetess who was sought after by the king for wisdom and counsel. She was highly esteemed.

Abigail was in a hopeless marriage to a churlish, evil liar. She behaved herself wisely even though her husband was wicked, and God rewarded her with a marriage to the king.

Sapphira, on the other hand, went along with her husband's lies, and they were both slain by God for conspiring to lie about how much they sold their property for.

Phoebe was a willing worker. She was both a servant and a leader as she helped those in leadership to minister to the Lord and to the people.

Lydia was a worshiper of God. She was full of hospitality. She opened her home for services. She was a businesswoman, a hard worker, faithful, and generous.

Mary Magdalene, once a harlot, "did what she could." She humbled herself before the Lord as she broke the alabaster box, pouring all that she owned upon His feet as she washed them with her tears and dried them with her hair.

Anna was a prophetess who lost her husband shortly after they were married. She dedicated herself to working for the Lord in the Temple, both day and night.

Mary hid God's word in her heart and raised her children to love, honor, and fear God. What an awesome responsibility she bore in having Jesus!

Dorcas was so important to the work of the Lord that when she died, the people begged Peter to come to pray for her that she would be brought back to life. And she was.

The mother of the disciples James and John was always trying to push Jesus to give her boys a better position. One commentary said they were called the "sons of thunder" because of their mother's reputation.

These women were just like us in so many ways. Some were single, some were married, some were widowed, some were wealthy, and some were poor. But all of them were brought to the kingdom of God for a purpose. Some fulfilled their purpose;

some did not.

Just as Esther was brought to the kingdom "for such a time as this," God has brought you to this time and place, in all of eternity, to make a difference in someone's life. He wants to use you to reach your family, your friends, and your community by being a Proverbs 31 lady:

- One who loves and fears God.
- One who has her priorities set God's way.
- One who works hard, is responsible, and not idle.
- One who is considerate of others and their needs.
- One who looks ahead and prepares for her family's needs.
- One who takes time to develop her own Christian character.
- One who is respected and loved by those around her.

Take time right now to ask God to help you be a Proverbs 31 lady, someone whom He can use in His kingdom as He fulfills His purpose in your life.

Capture Your Vapor

CHAPTER THIRTEEN

Capture Your Vapor

For what is your life? It is even a vapour, that appeareth for a little time, and then vanisheth away. (James 4:14)

*W*e know assuredly that this verse of Scripture is true. Our life span, be it seventy, eighty, or ninety years, when compared to the eons of time, is just like the steam that billows from your teapot. You see it for a few short seconds and then it is gone, never to be seen, felt, or heard again. Experience has shown us that when we harness this elusive substance, we are able to maneuver large steamships, power great locomotives, and heat huge buildings with relatively little effort. This steam, or vapor, when properly controlled, holds untold power.

What about the "vapor" of your life?

Is it under control, or do you feel that your life is like a runaway steam engine that is out of control? Do you feel frustrated by the endless challenges you seem to face every day? Would you like to get organized and relieve some of the stress in your life?

Years ago, I found that such a simple thing as writing was

just what I needed to put my life in order and harness my "vapor." Taking time to sit down and plan, organize, budget, schedule, set priorities and goals, and put my thoughts down was just what I needed to get my life organized and relieve stress.

I can hear you now, "Oh, but I can't write," or "That sounds like too much work for me," or "I wouldn't have any idea where to begin. . . ."

We wouldn't think of building a new home without making a very precise blueprint of every minute detail involved, material needed, cost estimated, and scheduled date of completion before that first shovelful of dirt is dug for the foundation. Why then do we build our lives differently? Why do we build them so haphazardly?

I Corinthians 14:40 admonished us to "Let all things be done decently and in order."

I have found that the best way for me to bring order to my life is to sit with a paper and pen and "order it!" Somehow it always seems things get put together faster, easier, and more precisely when I put it in writing first. A little premeditated thought can save a lot of time, energy, and effort.

This writing can take on many forms. For you it may begin with making lists. "I do make lists," I hear you say, but what do you do with them after you make them? Can you even remember where you put them and whether you wrote it on the back of an envelope, on a partially used napkin, or on the scrap of brown paper bag you tore off in a hurry? If you do make lists, begin with having a convenient place or container to keep them.

How many times have you spent the entire day running to and fro, trying to accomplish everything in one day, only to find that you either did a considerable amount of backtracking, forgot half the things you needed to get, or totally forgot the most important item of the day? Frustrating, wasn't it? It doesn't have to be!

Sit down. (Make the time.) List all you need to do and where you need to go. Then decide what your priorities are. What needs to be done first, second, third? Keep your plan intact. Take it with you and accomplish all you set out to do.

Take the time to set spiritual goals as well, and record your progress. Perhaps you've always wanted to read the Bible through. Write your goal and follow a daily reading plan that will help you accomplish your goal.

Writing has helped me organize my life and accomplish my goals. It has become a "silent friend" to help me sort out my fears and frustrations. It has helped me measure my spiritual progress.

Using a piece of paper as my "sounding board," rather than releasing my frustrations on my husband or family members, helps me stay in control of my emotions and helps me to reevaluate some things and get my priorities in line again.

Preserving memories has become one of my favorite reasons to write. Seeing the dates my children accomplished certain feats and what and how they said and did things brings back precious memories that would never have been preserved had I not taken the time to write them.

One year, as each child's birthday approached, I wrote his

or her life story up to the age of twelve years old. They thoroughly enjoyed reading about themselves as little children. Friends, pets, and exciting adventures they never remembered came to life as they read about them.

I read about one mother who kept spiral notebooks, one for each calendar year, and recorded all the family events, birthdays and holidays throughout her marriage. What a treasure as the children grew older and returned to sit by the fire as the mother related the many incidents that would otherwise have been totally forgotten!

Another avenue of writing that I have thoroughly enjoyed through the years is that of writing my prayers. It is awesome to record the date a prayer request is made and the date He brings it to pass. I had been praying for nearly twelve years that my mother would be filled with the Holy Spirit. Just two weeks after I wrote it with my prayer requests, she received the baptism of the Holy Spirit! Believe me, there was no magic in the fact that I had just written it, but it was fantastic anyway!

I've also enjoyed writing my prayers as I prayed through the Word, much like David in the Psalms:

"Lord let my delight be in Thy law, let me meditate on it day and night. Let me be like a tree that's planted by the rivers that bringeth forth fruit in his season. Don't let me falter or wither. Thou, O Lord, art a shield for me. My glory, and the uplifter of my soul. O Lord, how excellent is Thy name!"

Recording the many miracles, both large and small, that God so graciously bestows on us is another item that deserves attention. God has done so many special things for me: saving my mother, allowing my freezer to go out the week before the guarantee ran out, and allowing some dear soul to leave a short, stubby pencil to entertain my little one! Writing these things reminds us of His goodness to us.

It doesn't even hurt to write special compliments that have been given to you. My favorite one came from my husband. He had aspirations of becoming President before he found the Lord, and when he gave me the following compliment one day, I took it as a very high honor: "Hon, you would have made a great President's wife!"

Researchers have been studying journal writing, "expressive writing" as they call it, for more than twenty years. They have found that it helps people find meaning or come to terms with stressful events. James W. Pennebaker, Ph.D., a professor of psychology at the University of Texas at Austin and a leading authority on expressive writing, says that when we put troubles into words, "we're able to get past it. Once we move past it, we don't worry about it or obsess over it." Other research has shown that expressive writing can actually help to improve the physical health of the writer.

Who can write? Everyone! Especially you! Forget the grades you received in English class in composition or handwriting. Cultivate a fresh understanding of the power of the written word. Look at writing as a way to capture and express your vapor, your very life, harnessing it and putting it to use for you as only you can.

One of the nicest things about writing is that it is not an expensive hobby, yet it can be one of the most pleasurable and profitable experiences that you have ever encountered.

All you really need is a pen or pencil and paper. The paper need not be special, though I would caution you to use a notebook of some sort to maintain an ordered effect. I prefer a loose-leaf notebook because I like to move things around and I don't like to tear things out of a spiral notebook. Divider tabs are nice because they help you keep things more organized. (If you really want to "treat" yourself, purchase a fountain pen and a hand-tooled leather notebook!)

Whatever you do, try to keep your notes together and date each of them. I have many notes and poems from my early years that have no date on them, and they are written on every type of paper imaginable! Also, remember, if you find a poem or thought that someone else has written, be careful to give the author credit for it. Some of the things I so carefully preserved, I'm not really sure I wrote them!

Capture your vapor. It can help you become organized, help you to set priorities in your life, help you through a difficult period in your life, and give you the order your soul desires. Where would we be today if Matthew, Mark, Luke, and John had not captured the "vapor" of our Lord's life for us to know who He really is?

Get Real

CHAPTER FOURTEEN

Get Real

*I*f you keep up with the latest jargon, perhaps you remember the phrase "Get Real" that was popular several years ago.

The definition of the word "real" is: existing, in fact, actual, true, authentic, and genuine. God is real! He exists, He is actual, He is true, He is authentic.

When I think of "realness" in the Bible, I think of truth and righteousness. In John 14:6, Jesus said, "I am the way, the truth, and the life." Jesus spent the rest of the chapter telling His disciples who He was, explaining to them that if they had seen Him that they had seen the Father. He was clarifying to them that it was actually God Himself that was dwelling with them.

God has called us to His truth and His righteousness, and He wants us to be "real."

Do you remember the children's story entitled *The Velveteen Rabbit* by Margery Williams? It is the story of a little boy who received a velveteen rabbit in his Christmas stocking. The story says that for about two hours, the boy thought the rabbit was the best gift of all, the best toy he had ever received. Then company came over, more gifts were unwrapped, and the rabbit was quickly forgotten. He ended up in the nursery, as most toys do, and the only friend he had was the Skin Horse.

One day, he asked the Skin Horse, "What is REAL? Does it mean having things that buzz inside you and a stick-out handle?"

"'Real isn't how you are made,' said the Skin Horse. 'It's a thing that happens to you. . . . Generally, by the time you are Real, most of your hair has been loved off, . . . and you get . . . very shabby.'"

"'I suppose you are Real?' said the Rabbit."

The Skin Horse told him that the Boy's uncle had made him *real* many years ago. "Once you are Real, . . . it lasts for always."

The Rabbit thought it would be a long time before this magic called *real* happened to him.

If you remember the story, the little rabbit eventually become *real* because of the little boy's love.

There are some very powerful messages in this classic children's story that relate to us today as Christians.

Many people who become Christians are just like the little boy who thought the rabbit was the best gift of all and the best toy he had ever received, for about two hours. They are excited to be filled with the Holy Spirit and baptized in His name, but they allow the cares of life to draw their attention away from allowing Him to become real in their lives.

In Matthew, Jesus told the parable of the sower who went to sow seeds.

And he spake many things unto them in parables, saying, Behold, a sower went forth to sow; And when he sowed, some seeds fell by the way side, and the fowls came and devoured them up: Some fell upon stony places, where they had not much earth: and forthwith they sprung up, because they had no deepness of earth: And when the sun was up, they were scorched; and because they had no root, they withered away. And some fell among thorns; and the thorns sprung up, and choked them: But other fell into good ground, and brought forth fruit, some an hundredfold, some sixtyfold, some thirtyfold. Who hath ears to hear, let him hear. (Matthew 13:3-9)

He went on to interpret the parable to them:

Hear ye therefore the parable of the sower. When any one heareth the word of the kingdom, and understandeth it not, then cometh the wicked one, and catcheth away that which was sown in his heart. This is he which received seed by the way side. But he that received the seed into stony places, the same is he that heareth the word, and anon with joy receiveth it; Yet hath he not root in himself, but dureth for a while: for when tribulation or persecution ariseth because of the word, by and by he is offended. He also that received seed among the thorns is he that heareth the word; and the care of this world, and the deceitfulness of riches, choke the word, and he becometh unfruitful. But he that received seed into the good ground is he that heareth the

*word, and understandeth it; which also beareth fruit, and
bringeth forth, some an hundredfold, some sixty, some thirty.*
(Matthew 13:18-23)

The rabbit felt very insignificant and commonplace, just as
we do at times. He saw others who walked and buzzed, and
thought that if he was like them, he would be *real.*

The Skin Horse gave the Rabbit some excellent advice about
being *real.* He told him that being *real* is not how you are made;
"It's a thing that happens to you." We are not real when we are
in the world. In the world we are always trying to get someone's
attention by being what we think they want us to be. We try to
follow the latest fashions and fads because we want to fit in. But
when something happens to us, when we are filled with the baptism of the Holy Spirit and God begins to work on us, both inside
and out, we start to become *real.*

The Rabbit asked the Skin Horse some very deep questions,
"Does it hurt?"

"Sometimes . . . when you are Real you don't mind being
hurt," the Skin Horse told him.

"Does it happen all at once?" the Rabbit asked.

"You become. It takes a long time. That's why it doesn't
often happen to people who break easily, or have sharp edges, or
who have to be carefully kept. Generally, by the time you are
Real, most of your hair has been loved off, and your eyes drop
out and you get loose in the joints and very shabby. But these
things don't matter at all, because once you are Real you can't be

ugly, except to people who don't understand," the Skin Horse told him.

And isn't that how it is with us? Jesus wants us to be real. He wants us to desire to be real and He wants us to become real. But if we are a person who is easily offended, who cares that the changes God makes in us might make others look at us differently, then we will have a difficult time becoming real.

Sometimes being real hurts. Your hair may get rubbed off and your joints may get shabby, but you will never be ugly! Not to the Lord!

Jesus offended some people because of His lifestyle, and our being real Christians will offend some people.

And blessed is he, whosoever shall not be offended in me. (Matthew 11:6)

If the world hate you, ye know that it hated me before it hated you. (John 15:18)

When you are a real Christian you are not ashamed to follow His leading even though the world doesn't understand.

Being real means that
- you don't put on airs;
- you become as a little child who desires to grow up in Christ;
- you understand that you have no righteousness of yourself, and that you are only righteous because of Him;

- you realize your total dependence upon God;
- you need to allow yourself to be spent for the gospel. That you don't have to "buzz and tick and have a handle sticking out of your side" to be used by the Lord. That you can reach out to others when they are hurting and that it's okay to get your clothes and hands dirty as you help others;
- you need to accept yourself for who you are and who you are becoming in Christ, and not worry what others think;
- you need to prepare yourself now for what you feel God may use you for in the future.

God has a plan and a purpose for your life, if you will be like Paul, who said:

And I will very gladly spend and be spent for you; though the more abundantly I love you, the less I be loved. (II Corinthians 12:15)

Paul had a lot of head knowledge when he became a Christian, but he spent the first three years, after his conversion, in the desert to gain the heart knowledge he needed to truly be effective for Jesus.

To what is God calling you? The Scripture tells us to:

Study to shew thyself approved unto God, a workman that needeth not to be ashamed, rightly dividing the word of truth. (II Timothy 2:15)

Being real means reaching out to others in discipleship, being willing to take time with people. It means being real in relationships with our natural family and our spiritual family, with friends, with strangers, and with the Lord. It means not being afraid to say, "I'm sorry," and "Please forgive me." It means:

> *Let all bitterness, and wrath, and anger, and clamour, and evil speaking, be put away from you, with all malice: and be ye kind one to another, tenderhearted, forgiving one another, even as God for Christ's sake hath forgiven you.* (Ephesians 4:31-32)

In conclusion, being real means you are willing and desiring to grow in Christ, in His righteousness and in His Spirit. Remember, "Being Real doesn't happen all at once. It takes a long time. . . ." Don't expect your spiritual growth to take place overnight. Allow God to mold you and make you into the vessel He desires you to be.

Artificial plants may be easy to care for, but they never grow. They're not real, real things grow, get *real*!

Three
Magic
Words

CHAPTER FIFTEEN

Three Magic Words

This know also, that in the last days perilous times shall come. For men shall be lovers of their own selves, covetous, boasters, proud, blasphemers, disobedient to parents, unthankful, unholy, without natural affection, trucebreakers, false accusers, incontinent, fierce, despisers of those that are good, traitors, heady, highminded, lovers of pleasures more than lovers of God; having a form of godliness, but denying the power thereof: from such turn away. (II Timothy 3:1-5)

Truly these verses of Scripture describe the day in which we live. Verse two mentions "unthankful" as a sign of the last days. I don't know about you, but have you noticed in the last few years how unthankful people are? You do something really nice for them or say something complimentary to them, and they don't respond at all or there is a grunt. You hold a door open for them, allow them to go ahead of you in line, or allow them to move through an intersection first, and they don't even acknowledge your kindness.

We've seen people come into the church, whose lives God

has completely changed and delivered and people who have been healed from life-threatening diseases who just turn their back on God and walk away. We've seen marriages God has restored and children who have returned to their families, and they just walked away. We've seen people to whom the church has ministered in times of financial and emotional needs, who were ungrateful and unthankful, even to the point of saying it wasn't enough, they needed more. They are unthankful, just as Timothy said. We live in an "entitlement" culture. "Gimme, gimme, take, take, take," as one children's song said years ago.

As Christians, we should be the most thankful people in the world. We should always have a thankful heart towards people. We need to look for the small things for which to thank people, going out of our way to let people know that we appreciate what they did for us, be it little or big! If someone compliments you, learn to say "thank you." Don't try to put yourself down or try to make some disclaimer, trying to appear humble; simply say, "thank you." The world needs to see us as a thankful people! It definitely is not the norm today.

Thankfulness has always been a key element in worshiping God. Sacrifice and offerings are to be made with thanksgiving, not grudgingly. David loved to sing songs of thankfulness to God. He thanked God for the good things and the bad things. In the Old Testament, regiments were assigned to do nothing but worship God in thankfulness. God is no different than we are; He wants to know that we appreciate what He does for us.

Thanksgiving is a natural element of Christian worship and

should characterize all of the Christian life. We should learn to thank God for everything, even the things that cause us problems. I Thessalonians 5:18 "In every thing give thanks: for this is the will of God in Christ Jesus concerning you."

In *The Hiding Place*, Corrie ten Boom shared an amazing story about being thankful. Her entire Dutch family had been imprisoned in Nazi concentration camps for hiding Jews. At one point she and her sister were moved to Ravensbruk, which was overcrowded and flea infested. She felt it was the worst of all the camps they had been in, and she hated it from the first day. When they had their daily devotions, her sister Betsy said that they needed to pray and to thank God for their new living quarters like the Scriptures said in I Thessalonians 5:18. Corrie said that she could not bring herself to thank God for the fleas, but finally she did, at Betsy's insistence. From the very beginning at Ravensbruk, they were amazed to find how freely they were able to hold Bible studies and prayer meetings. The guards never stopped them like they had in other camps. Months later she found out that the guards would not go into their living quarters because of the fleas! Corrie was so happy that she had thanked God for the fleas when she understood how they had protected them from having to stop preaching and teaching the Word of God.

A couple of years ago, I heard about a man in China who was imprisoned for becoming a Christian. Every day he volunteered to work in the latrines and at the water treatment plant where no one else would go. He chose that assignment because there he was free to worship and praise God all day long and no one made him stop because no one else would go near the place! He could sing, he could shout, he could worship however he wanted, and no one would stop him. He thanked God every day that he had the opportunity to worship and praise Him! Oh, that we would worship God the same way, considering the freedom that we have!

When we were little children, our parents taught us to say the "three magic words." What were they? "Please" and "thank you." Just because we're grown-up now doesn't mean we don't need to still say those words!

We need to have them ever ready on our lips to show our appreciation to God for the many wonderful things He does for us every day, to each other and to everyone we meet. People will know we are different if we truly show appreciation for what they do for us.

Therefore will I give thanks unto thee, O LORD, among the heathen, and sing praises unto thy name. (Psalm 18:49)

So we thy people and sheep of thy pasture will give thee thanks for ever: we will shew forth thy praise to all generations. (Psalm 79:13)

Ye also helping together by prayer for us, that for the gift bestowed upon us by the means of many persons thanks may be given by many on our behalf. (II Corinthians 1:11)

One hundred and thirty-two verses of Scripture mention some form of the word "thanks." I believe the Lord is trying to tell us something!

Consider the Lily Work

CHAPTER SIXTEEN

Consider the Lily Work

*H*ave you ever wondered why God does things the way He does? I am always so amazed when I look at the sky on a clear night. The stars are just beautiful. Totally breathtaking! And yet the Scripture declares their creation very simply in Genesis 1:16 "And God made two great lights; the greater light to rule the day, and the lesser light to rule the night: *he made the stars also*" (emphasis mine).

I take that to mean that it didn't take any effort at all for the Lord to make them, almost as if they were an afterthought.

If you've ever been to an aquarium where they have saltwater fish, you see magnificently colored fish that God has hidden deep in the expanse of the ocean, never to be seen naturally by human eyes.

I would have to say: the Lord is detail oriented!

When Solomon began to build the Temple, he was concerned that the finest craftsmen living would do the work. He hired artisans who took their time and paid attention to details because it was a work that was to be presented to Jehovah, a place designed to worship the almighty God!

And king Solomon sent and fetched Hiram out of Tyre. He was a widow's son of the tribe of Naphtali, and his father was a man of Tyre, a worker in brass: and he was filled with wisdom, and understanding, and cunning to work all works in brass. And he came to king Solomon, and wrought all his work. For he cast two pillars of brass, of eighteen cubits high apiece: and a line of twelve cubits did compass either of them about. And he made two chapiters of molten brass, to set upon the tops of the pillars: the height of the one chapiter was five cubits, and the height of the other chapiter was five cubits: And nets of checker work, and wreaths of chain work, for the chapiters which were upon the top of the pillars; seven for the one chapiter, and seven for the other chapiter. And he made the pillars, and two rows round about upon the one network, to cover the chapiters that were upon the top, with pomegranates: and so did he for the other chapiter. And the chapiters that were upon the top of the pillars were of lily work in the porch, four cubits. And the chapiters upon the two pillars had pomegranates also above, over against the belly which was by the network: and the pomegranates were two hundred in rows round about upon the other chapiter. And he set up the pillars in the porch of the temple: and he set up the right pillar, and called the name thereof Jachin: and he set up the left pillar, and he called the name thereof Boaz. And upon the top of the pillars was lily work: so was the work of the pillars finished. (I Kings 7:13-22)

In these verses of Scripture, we see that brass pillars were intricately molded and sculpted to be placed between the Temple and the court of the priests, for seemingly no useful purpose other than to be ornamental. They were pillars that were approximately twenty-seven feet high, eighteen feet around and made of metal three to four inches thick. Sitting on the top of each pillar there were capitals or 'chapiters' that were eight feet tall. (The study of architecture reveals that each period of time or culture developed its own style of capitals, the top part of a pillar or column.)

When Hiram cast the capital, he made it either in the shape of a lily, or he made it plain and etched a design of lilies (lily work) on it. Then the Scriptures tell us he covered the chapiter with seven nets of finely woven brass and then two rows of pomegranates with two hundred pomegranates in each row. In essence, what he did was totally cover the intricate lily work. Had it not been recorded that the lily work was at the top of each pillar, no one would even have known it was there except the Lord, because it was totally hidden from the view of man.

All of that work done with precision and intricacy, only to be hidden by network and pomegranates. To the natural man, it really doesn't make sense, but the lilies had a prophetic role. The lilies represented Jesus. Jesus, who at that time was hidden from view, stood symbolically over the very entrance to the Temple that the priests had to pass through daily!

Jesus is referred to as a lily in Song of Solomon 2:1 "I am the rose of Sharon, and the lily of the valleys." (I think this verse is

175

often misquoted. It doesn't say "lily of the valley"; it says "lily of the valleys," helping us to realize that regardless how many spiritual valleys we go through, He is the lily of every one of them!)

Lilies have always been a symbol of purity. What is more pure than our Lord and Savior Jesus Christ?

Perhaps the Lord likened Himself to the trumpet-shaped lily because it reminds Him of the trumpet that will sound when He returns to take us, His bride, home!

Jesus referred to lilies when He talked about our need to have faith and trust in Him.

And why take ye thought for raiment? Consider the lilies of the field, how they grow; they toil not, neither do they spin: and yet . . . Solomon in all his glory was not arrayed like one of these. (Matthew 6:28-29)

Our lives need to be like the lilies, intricately designed and sculpted by the Master, yet hidden from view. We should not be in front taking glory for our spiritual "beauty" and how much we do for God, but we should do a work for the Lord that many times is hidden from the view of human eyes.

When we talk to someone about the Lord, we don't know if we are being used to plant a seed or water, and we may never know the extent of the increase that God will give. When we cultivate others by encouraging them, giving advice, or ministering to them, people may never see what we have done, and we may never know what we have done, but God does. Even though it may appear to be hidden from view, God sees and it is recorded.

The night that I received the baptism of the Holy Spirit, my soul was "ripe unto harvest." Not one person that night invited me to seek after the Lord. Not one person witnessed to me that night. My soul was thirsty and hungry from seeds that had been planted and watered for many years by countless others who had been developing the lily work in their lives: praying, witnessing, and teaching the Word of God, not expecting any glory in return, knowing that what they had done in secret, God would one day openly reward!

History tells us that Leonardo da Vinci dedicated three years to his famous painting of The Last Supper. Before he unveiled the painting to the public, he decided to show it to a friend for whose opinion he had the utmost respect.

His friend was profusely lavish in his praise. "The cup in Jesus' hand," he said, "is especially beautiful."

Da Vinci immediately began to paint out the cup. The friend was astonished! He felt the picture was beautiful just the way it was. He didn't understand. He demanded an explanation.

"Nothing," da Vinci explained, "must distract from the figure of Christ."

And so it should be with us. Nothing in our life should distract us from Jesus. All the praise and all the glory of anything we do for Christ needs to be directed back to Him. And nothing in our life should distract others from seeing Jesus in us.

What Are You Willing to Pay?

CHAPTER SEVENTEEN

What Are You Willing to Pay?

F don't know about you, but to me, Christmas is a very special time of the year. It's a very busy time, a time of much preparation, and a time of following longstanding family traditions, but it is also a time of reflection.

It's a time to send cards and letters to people we may not see or hear from all year. A time to keep in touch, reviving old memories and making new ones.

There are certain sounds and even smells associated with Christmas. Christmas carols, bells ringing, pine, bayberry, cinnamon, and peppermint, all draw your senses into the season. Holly, poinsettias, evergreens, lights, wreaths, decorations. . . .

It's a time of celebrating family traditions that bind people together and help them remember that they are a part of each other. I find myself digging out old family recipes that are used only once or twice a year, remembering the hours my mother and my aunt Mary baked endless dozens of cookies for Christmas.

It's a busy, busy time with all the dinners, parties, family gatherings, and of course all the shopping!

We always say we'll spend less each year, but we never do. We're looking for just the right gift to make someone happy. We want to buy something they will really like, something that they will value and appreciate, something that won't be buried in a closet, hidden in a cupboard, or be donated to the next white elephant sale. We want to buy something they will remember us by.

Christmas shoppers are interesting. Some will only shop at certain stores, some will only purchase brand-name items. Some shoppers won't buy an item unless it is on sale, and some never look at the price tag. Most of us check to see that there is some type of warranty or guarantee on the product in case it is faulty or the recipient doesn't like it and it needs to be returned.

Then there's the wrapping! The list just goes on and on with all the preparations for Christmas.

This year, as you're thinking and planning for all of the gifts, think of what gift you will give Jesus, both this year and the rest of your life. After all, it is His birthday!

We know that we could never "pay" for our salvation, but if we did have to pay for it, what do you think it might cost?

What are you willing to pay for it in your time, energy, or finances?

Harold Sala once told about a man who was walking by some store windows during the Christmas season. One particular jewelry store caught his attention with their beautiful display. There were cross necklaces, earrings, and pins for sale. Some were solid diamonds, some were studded with emeralds or embellished with rubies. All were set in gold or sterling silver, and they were beautiful. He was enjoying the glistening beauty when a sign in the corner, by the window, caught his eye. "All on Easy Terms" the sign read. And it occurred to the man that many Christians want the beauty of Christianity and its salvation in their lives, but they are not willing to pay the price. They want God, His many blessings, and salvation, "All on Easy Terms."

David once made the mistake of numbering Israel, and the Lord instructed the prophet to give David three options to make things right. Of the three options, David chose to fall into the hands of God and His mercy. David was instructed to build an altar to God and to repent of his wrongdoing.

The prophet told David where the altar needed to be built, and David, the king himself, went to the owner of the land to ask if he could purchase it. Now mind you, David was king at the time. He could have sent a servant, a soldier, or even his treasurer to make the purchase, but he went shopping on his own!

When he got there, the landowner Arunah was so overwhelmed at the king's presence and humility in explaining his need to purchase a piece of his land, that Arunah offered to give King David the land. He not only offered to give the threshing floor to David, but he also offered him the oxen that trod there as well as his own tools and plows to be used in the sacrifice David was to make to atone for his sin. Many would have jumped at the chance! David could have thought, "Wow! God has provided all of this, and I don't even have to pay for it."

But that wasn't David's reply. David told Arunah that he couldn't offer anything to God that had cost him nothing. I have a feeling that, in the end, David probably paid more for the land than it was even worth! I believe the price that he paid was a sacrifice, something that cost him something.

At Christmas, we usually think of Mary. Her joy must have been great when the angel of the Lord came to her and told her that she had been chosen among women to bear the Messiah. But we don't often think of the sacrifices that she ultimately made because she was the chosen one.

When the angel spoke to her, she was espoused, engaged, to Joseph, and in those days, to break an engagement you had to get a divorce! When Joseph found out that she was "with child," that is exactly what he was going to do, to have her "put away privately." He loved Mary, but he was a respectable man. He knew he wasn't the father. The law said that he could have had her stoned! In the angel's pronouncement, Mary actually risked having the man she loved kill her!

After all, they had wedding plans made. What would people think? Many feel that Joseph was an older man who was probably settled and had his own carpenter shop. He had the promise of the "good life." All he needed was a wife to begin his family. He certainly wouldn't want to ruin his life by marrying someone who was unfaithful to him even before they married.

Joseph must have been a very devout man, because he too was chosen by God to raise Jesus. So when the angel spoke to Joseph and he understood what was going on, he quickly took Mary in. Then the odyssey began.

They had to go to Bethlehem for the child to be born and

then they had to flee to Egypt to spare the baby's life. At Jesus' circumcision, Simeon warned Mary that her heart would be pierced many times over because of this child.

During His ministry, Jesus was mocked and thought to be a lunatic. As a mother Mary must have suffered to see her son treated this way. His public death on the cross had to be the greatest insult a mother could bear. Everyone knew only the worst offenders were hung on a cross, yet Scripture tells us that she stood by the cross through it all, affirming her commitment and her faith that the man hanging there was the same one who the angel told her would save all men from their sins. She never doubted! She never gave up!

Oh, what sacrifices she made to give of herself to the Lord! Certainly it cost her something.

What sacrifices are you willing to make to give yourself to the Lord? Time? Energy? Commitment? Obedience to His Word? Are you willing to sacrifice the pleasures of sin for a season, knowing the eternal rewards you will reap? Can you give yourself wholly to God in worship, not just in lip service? Can you lay aside traditions taught by men and study the Scriptures for yourself to find biblical truth?

Search the scriptures; for in them ye think ye have eternal life: and they are they which testify of me. (John 5:39)

Study to shew thyself approved unto God, a workman that needeth not to be ashamed, rightly dividing the word of truth. (II Timothy 2:15)

There are no easy terms to salvation! It does cost you something, but what more could you ask for?

Jesus is "name brand":

> *Neither is there salvation in any other: for there is none other name under heaven given among men, whereby we must be saved.* (Acts 4:12)

Whether you look at the price tag or not, nothing could ever pay for the blessings that belong to a child of God! No need to comparison shop. There is none like the Lord!

If warranties or guarantees concern you, there are no warranties or promises like the Lord's! His are everlasting! His promises are out of this world! Satisfaction guaranteed!

Jesus is the best gift you can give yourself! Won't you seek Him with your whole heart and allow Him to baptize you in His Spirit and into His death, burial, and resurrection as you are immersed in His name as Acts 2:38 tells us? "Then Peter said unto them, Repent, and be baptized every one of you in the name of Jesus Christ for the remission of sins, and ye shall receive the gift of the Holy Ghost."

It is the gift that truly keeps on giving!

APPENDIX

The Meanest Mother
Written by: Bobbie Pingaro, 1967
Unabridged version

J had the meanest mother in the whole world. While other kids ate candy for breakfast, I had to have cereal, eggs or toast. When others had Cokes and cookies for lunch, I had to eat a sandwich. As you can guess, my supper was different than the other kids also. But at least I wasn't alone in my sufferings. My sister and two brothers had the same mean mother as I did.

My mother insisted upon knowing where we were at all times. You'd think we were on a chain gang. She had to know who our friends were and where we were going. She insisted if we said we'd be gone an hour, that we be gone one hour or less—not one hour and one minute. I am nearly ashamed to admit it, but she actually struck us. Not once, but each time we had a mind of our own and did as we pleased. That poor belt was used more on our seats than it was to hold up Daddy's pants. Can you imagine someone actually hitting a child just because he disobeyed?

Now you can begin to see how mean she really was.

We had to wear clean clothes and take a bath. The other kids always wore their clothes for days. We reached the height of insults because she made our clothes herself, just to save money. Why, oh, why did we have to have a mother who made us feel different from our friends? The worst is yet to come. We had to be in bed by nine each night and up at eight the next morning. We couldn't sleep till noon like our friends. So while they slept, my mother actually had the nerve to break the child labor law. She made us work. We had to wash dishes, make beds, learn to cook and all sorts of cruel things. I believe she laid awake at night thinking up mean things to do to us.

She always insisted upon us telling the truth, the whole truth and nothing but the truth, even if it killed us—and it nearly did. By the time we were teenagers, she was much wiser, and our life became even more unbearable. None of this tooting the horn of a car for us to come running. She embarrassed us to no end by making our dates and friends come to the door to get us. If I spent the night with a girlfriend, can you imagine she checked on me to see if I was really there? I never had the chance to elope to Mexico. That is, if I'd had a boyfriend to elope with. I forgot to mention, while my friends were dating at the age of twelve and thirteen, my old-fashioned mother refused to let me date until the age of fifteen and sixteen. Fifteen, that is, if you dated only to go to a school function. And that was maybe twice a year.

Through the years, things didn't improve a bit. We could not lie in bed "sick" like our friends did and miss school. If our friends had a toe ache, a hangnail or serious ailment, they could stay home from school. Our marks in school had to be up to par.

Our friends' report cards had beautiful colors on them, black for passing, red for failing. My mother, being as different as she was, would settle for nothing less than ugly black marks.

As the years rolled by, first one and then the other of us was put to shame. We were graduated from high school. With our mother behind us, talking, hitting and demanding respect, none of us was allowed the pleasure of being a dropout. My mother was a complete failure as a mother. Out of four children, a couple of us attained some higher education. None of us have ever been arrested, or beaten his mate. Each of my brothers served his time in the service of this country.

And whom do we have to blame for the terrible way we turned out? You're right, our mean mother. Look at the things we missed. We never got to march in a protest parade, nor to take part in a riot, burn draft cards, and a million and one other things that our friends (did). She forced us to grow up into God-fearing, educated, honest adults. Using this as a background I am trying to raise my three children. I stand a little taller and I am filled with pride when my children call me mean. Because, you see, I thank God He gave me the meanest mother in the whole world.